Judaism

Religions of the World

Series Editor: Ninian Smart

Judaism

Dan Cohn-Sherbok

University of Wales

LONDON

First published in Great Britain 1999
by Routledge
11 New Fetter Lane, London EC4P 4EE

ISBN 0-415-21345-2 (hbk)
ISBN 0-415-21164-6 (pbk)

This book was designed and produced by Calmann & King Ltd, London

Editorial work by Melanie White and Damian Thompson
Pronunciation guide by Heather Gross
Design by Design Deluxe and Karen Stafford
Maps by Andrea Fairbrass
Artworks by Sarah-Jayne Stafford
Picture research by Peter Kent
Printed in China

Reviewer Alford T. Welch, Michigan State University

Picture Credits

Cover Nigel Howard, Hutchison Library; *page 17* Barnaby's Picture
Library; *42* Studio Canali; *46* German Archeological Institute;
58 AKG London; *73* J.C. Tordai/Panos Pictures; *88* Juliette
John/Barnaby's Picture Library; *91* Liba Taylor, Hutchison Library;
106 Facelly/Sipa Press

Contents

Foreword

Religions of the World

The informed citizen or student needs a good overall knowledge of our small but complicated world. Fifty years ago you might have neglected religions. Now, however, we are shrewder and can see that religions and ideologies not only form civilizations but directly influence international events. These brief books provide succinct, balanced, and informative guides to the major faiths and one volume also introduces the changing religious scene as we enter the new millennium.

Today we want not only to be informed, but to be stimulated by the life and beliefs of the diverse and often complicated religions of today's world. These insightful and accessible introductions allow you to explore the riches of each tradition—to understand its history, its beliefs and practices, and also to grasp its influence upon the modern world. The books have been written by a team of excellent and, on the whole, younger scholars who represent a new generation of writers in the field of religious studies. While aware of the political and historical influences of religion these authors aim to present the religion's spiritual side in a fresh and interesting way. So whether you are interested simply in descriptive knowledge of a faith, or in exploring its spiritual message, you will find these introductions invaluable.

The emphasis in these books is on the modern period, because every religious tradition has transformed itself in the face of the traumatic experiences of the last two hundred years or more. Colonialism, industrialization, nationalism, revivals of religion, new religions, world wars, revolutions, social transformations have not left faith unaffected and have drawn on religious and anti-religious forces to reshape our world. Modern technology in the last 25 years—from the Boeing 747 to the world wide web—has made our globe seem a much smaller place. Even the moon's magic has been captured by technology.

We meet in these books people of the modern period as a sample of the many changes over the last few centuries. At the same time, each book provides a valuable insight into the different dimensions of the religion: its teachings, narratives, organizations, rituals, and experiences. In touching on these features, each volume gives a rounded view of the tradition enabling you to understand what it means to belong to a particular faith. As the Native American proverb has it: "Never judge a person without walking a mile in his moccasins."

To assist you further in your exploration, several useful reference aids are included. Each book contains a chronology, map, glossary, pronunciation guide, list of festivals, annotated reading list, and index. A selection of images provide examples of religious art, symbols, and contemporary practices. Focus boxes explore in more detail the relation between the faith and some aspect of the arts—whether painting, sculpture, architecture, literature, dance, or music.

I hope you will find these introductions enjoyable and illuminating. Brevity is supposed to be the soul of wit: it can also turn out to be what we need in the first instance in introducing cultural and spiritual themes.

Ninian Smart
Santa Barbara, 1998

Preface

Growing up in the leafy suburbs of Denver, Colorado, I was exposed to two very different worlds: a typical American high school and, in the afternoon and on weekends, a Jewish religion school. Later I was a student at Williams College in the mountains of Massachusetts—a very Gentile environment—and subsequently studied at the Hebrew Union College–Jewish Institute of Religion, an intensive Jewish environment. Once I qualified as a Reform rabbi, I moved to England where I was a student at Cambridge University, an institution deeply influenced by its Christian heritage, and have taught Jewish studies in Canterbury and now in Wales. During all this time, I have struggled to integrate the Jewish tradition with the demands of modern life.

This is the central dilemma facing Jews today, and it is the aim of this book to highlight the perplexities of remaining Jewish in our highly secularized world. Beginning with an account of Jewish life in the suburbs, the book goes on to explore the nature of the Jewish religious establishment, the State of Israel, the question of who is a Jew, and the character of the Jewish community worldwide. This discussion sets the stage for an account of the history of the Jewish people from biblical times to the present. This is followed by an outline of the basic beliefs and practices within Orthodox and non-Orthodox Judaism.

Turning to the creation of a Jewish homeland, the final chapter raises fundamental questions about the direction of Israel in the next century, and examines major challenges to Judaism in the future. Throughout readers are encouraged to ponder the issues facing Jews on the threshold of a new millennium. Orthodox Jewish theology, traditional Jewish practice, the divine status of the *Torah*, the ancient definition of Jewishness, the age-old role of women, the political state of Israel, and the primacy of the Jewish faith are all being questioned. If the Jewish people are not to become extinct, these problems must be confronted. What is at stake is no less than the survival of Judaism as a living religion.

Dan Cohn-Sherbok
April 1988

Chronology of Judaism

B.C.E.	Event
c. 2000–1750	Era of the Patriarchs (Abraham, Isaac, Jacob).
c. 1750	Jacob's family settle in Egypt.
18th century	First mention of "Apiru," possible forerunners of the Hebrews, in texts found in Mari.
17th/16th century	Rule of Asiatic Hyksos dynasty in Egypt.
13th/12th century	Exodus from Egypt. Settlement in Canaan. Era of the Judges.
11th century	Establishment of the Monarchy under King Saul.
10th century	Era of King David and the conquest of Jerusalem. Era of King Solomon and the building of the First Temple.
c. 930	Death of King Solomon and the division of the Kingdom.
Mid 9th century	Era of the prophets Elijah and Elisha.
c. 840	Black Obelisk showing King Jehu bowing to Assyria.
8th century	Era of the prophets Amos, Hosea, Micah, and Isaiah.
Late 8th century	Reform of cult by King Hezekiah of Judah.
Late 7th century	King Josiah's reforms. Deuteronomy, one of the five Books of Moses, is discovered.
721	Northern Kingdom falls to Assyria.

586	The Ten Northern Tribes deported. Destruction of First Temple in Jerusalem by Babylonians.
586-538	Exile of Jews to Babylon.
538	Return to Jerusalem and rebuilding of the Temple.
5th century	Religious renewal led by the scribe Ezra.
4th/3rd century	Judaea falls within the ambit of the Persian, then Macedonian, then Egyptian empires.
198	Judaea taken over by the Seleucid dynasty.
164	Maccabean revolt. Precarious independence established.
63	Judaea becomes part of the Roman Empire.
37-4 B.C.E. *	Reign of King Herod. Temple rebuilt.
1st century C.E. *	Era of the Pharisees, Sadducees, and Essenes.
70	Second Temple of Jerusalem destroyed during the Jewish War.
132-35	Rebellion of Simeon bar Kochba ends in failure.
Late 1st century	Establishment of rabbinic academy at Javneh.
3rd century	Compilation of *Mishnah* by Judah ha-Nasi.
Late 4th century	Compilation of the Jerusalem *Talmud*.
6th century	Compilation of the Babylonian *Talmud*.
8th century	Emergence of Karaites.

B.C.E. indicates Before the Common Era.   C.E. indicates the Common Era.

c. 800	Pact of Omar regulates lives of Jews in Islamic Empire.
9th/10th century	Jewish life spreads to Europe, North Africa, and Iraq.
10th-12th century	Golden Age of Spanish Jewry.
1096	Massacre of Rhineland Jews during the First Crusade.
Late 11th century	Compilation of Rashi's Biblical commentaries.
1144	First instance of the Blood Libel in Norwich, England.
Mid 12th century	Philosopher Maimonides produces codification of Jewish law.
1291	Expulsion of Jews from England.
13th century on	Jews of Poland protected.
Late 13th century	Emergence of *Zohar* and the mystical tradition.
1492	Jews expelled from Spain.
16th century	Revival of mystical tradition in Safed, Palestine.
17th/18th century	Jews in Eastern Europe suffer many changes.
1648	Chmielnicki massacre in Poland/Lithuania.
1666	Shabbetai Zevi converts to Islam.
Early 18th century	Emergence of *Hasidism* in Eastern Europe.
Mid 18th century	Jewish Enlightenment (Moses Mendelssohn).

18th/19th century	Jews increasingly granted civil rights in Western Europe.
19th century	Growth of Reform movement in Western Europe and USA.
1818	First Reform synagogue built in Hamburg, Germany.
1875	Hebrew Union College opens in Cincinnati.
1880-1920	Pogroms against Jews in Eastern Europe. Mass emigration to United States.
1896	Dreyfus case in France.
1897	Theodor Herzl convenes First Zionist Congress in Basle.
1919	League of Nations agrees Britain should administer Palestine.
1933-1945	Nazi anti-semitism leads to murder of six million Jews in Europe.
1948	Establishment of the State of Israel.
1967	Jerusalem reunited in Six Day War. Israel gains control of the West Bank, Gaza Strip, and the Golan Heights.
1970s on	Reform movement ordains women as rabbis.
1990s	Thousands of Russian Jews emigrate to Israel.
1993	Peace talks between Israeli government and Palestine Liberation Organization.
1995	Assassination of Prime Minister Yitzhak Rabin.

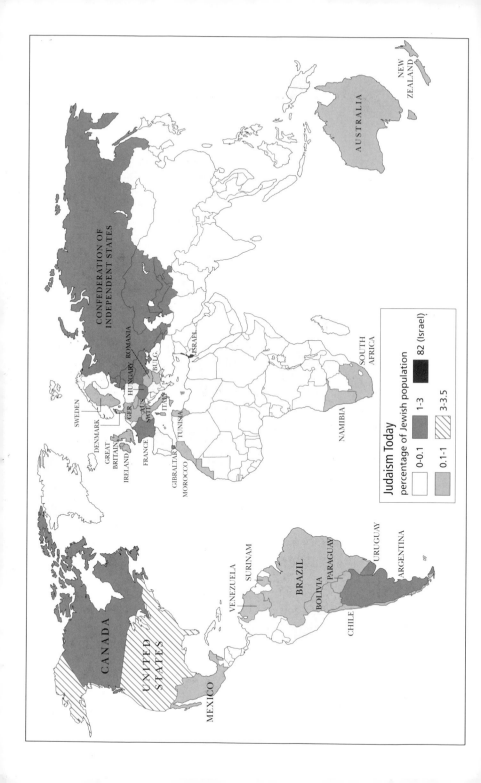

Judaism Today

percentage of Jewish population

- ☐ 0–0.1
- ☐ 0.1–1
- ☐ 1–3
- ☐ 3–3.5
- ■ 82 (Israel)

CONFEDERATION OF
INDEPENDENT STATES

SWEDEN
DENMARK
GREAT BRITAIN
IRELAND
FRANCE
GER.
AUS.
SWITZ.
ITALY
HUNGARY
ROMANIA
BULG.
ISRAEL
GIBRALTAR
MOROCCO
TUNISIA

SOUTH AFRICA
NAMIBIA

AUSTRALIA
NEW ZEALAND

CANADA
UNITED STATES
MEXICO
VENEZUELA
SURINAM
BRAZIL
BOLIVIA
PARAGUAY
CHILE
URUGUAY
ARGENTINA

Sabbath in the Suburbs

Genesis, the first book in the Jews' Hebrew Bible, states that in the course of six days God made heaven and earth, and created "Man in His image." Then on the seventh day God rested, and this has been known ever since as the **Sabbath**. When Moses received the **Ten Commandments**, God again commanded the Israelites, "Remember the Sabbath, and keep it holy."

The Sabbath—which in the Jewish tradition begins on Friday evening and ends on Saturday evening—is considered the holiest day of the year (with the possible exception of **Yom Kippur**, the Day of Atonement), even though it occurs 52 times every 12 months. Christians, too, accept the notion of the Sabbath, but celebrate it on Sundays.

There are many different ways of observing the Sabbath in the Jewish community. The following is an eyewitness account of a Friday evening spent with a strictly **Orthodox** family.

It was a summer Friday evening in the suburb of a large American city. The houses were not large, but they were well kept and were shaded by carefully planted trees. Everywhere automatic sprinklers played so the surrounding grass was green and lush. This was an Orthodox Jewish neighborhood and the Sabbath was about to begin.

Groups of men and boys were making their way by foot to the **synagogue**, dressed in their Sabbath best. Despite the heat, they wore dark jackets and trousers and their heads were covered either with small skull caps or with capacious black hats. Most were bearded and their white ritual **fringes** were visible outside their trousers. Among the procession was the **rabbi**, magnificent in black hat and shiny kaftan, leading his two sons by their hands.

Meanwhile the houses were abuzz with activity. Even in the rabbi's home hairdryers hummed, children shouted and stamped, and there was a constant sound of running feet. There was a sense of urgency; [a telephone call must be returned immediately because, according to Jewish law, once the Sabbath begins the telephone must remain silent.] In the dining room dinner had been laid for twenty people. Two non-Jewish women were making extensive preparations in the kitchen. Then all the women of the household suddenly appeared. The rabbi's wife accompanied by her mother and sister were all exquisitely dressed and their heads covered with elegantly styled wigs. [Jewish law lays down that married women must cover their heads] and it has become a tradition in many Orthodox communities that this commandment is fulfilled by wearing a wig. There were three little girls in long party frocks and three small boys, two of whom were still babies.

The other female guests consisted of an elderly Russian woman with her daughter and granddaughter. They had arrived in the United States from St. Petersburg earlier that very day. The rabbi had immediately invited them to spend the Sabbath at his house. None of them could speak a word of English, but another Russian woman who had been in the country for a year had come with them. There was also an English journalist present, who was writing a book on the Jewish community of the city. Of all the women, she was not Orthodox, but in respect for her host and hostess, she had completely covered her hair with a large scarf.

[The women then lit Sabbath candles and said the traditional Sabbath blessing in Hebrew: "Blessed art Thou, O Lord our God, King of the Universe, who hast sanctified us by Thy Commandments and commanded us to light the Sabbath lights." There must have been 30 candles and the table was ablaze when the men returned from synagogue. "Good **Shabbos**, good *Shabbos*!" they said to the women. Others called out to each other the purer Hebrew greeting—Shabbat Shalom—a peaceful Sabbath. Besides all the husbands, there were various nephews and a couple of young rabbinical students from the local **Yeshiva** (*Talmudic* academy).

The rabbi took his seat at one end of the table with his father-in-law at the other. The blessing over a cup of wine was said by every man present, one after the other. The Sabbath songs were led by the younger son-in-law and only the men sang. According to the strictest interpretation of Orthodox Jewish law, it is against the law for men to listen to women singing so the women sat quietly and enjoyed the music. Then the food was served. It was a feast. There was *gefilte* fish (fish patties), chicken

At the Sabbath dinner, the head of the family recites the blessing over bread: "Blessed art thou, O Lord our God, king of the universe, who brings forth bread from the earth."

soup with dumplings, roasted chicken, breadcrumbed chicken, sweet chicken, apple *kugel* (pudding), potato *kugel*, onion *kugel*, and a huge salad of tomato and cucumber. The food was strictly *kosher*. The chicken had been ritually and humanely slaughtered by a qualified butcher. Strict Jewish food law decrees that milk and meat should not be served together; so, because it was a meat meal, no dairy products were served and dessert was a non-dairy ice cream. The Russian women were amazed that such a thing existed.

It was a long, long meal. The rabbi's wife, with her mother and sister, served the men and scarcely sat down. Meanwhile the two **Gentile** women in the kitchen were busy with the washing up and with taking yet more food out of the oven while the masculine singing continued. After no more could be eaten, the traditional grace after the meal was sung. At long last everyone dispersed. The journalist, who lived on the other side of the city, was staying the night in the house as Jewish law forbids all motorized travel on the Sabbath. She and her husband sat and chatted with the father-in-law, who was a remarkable person. He had grown up in only a moderately Orthodox home and he had been educated at Harvard University. But after his marriage he had been determined to provide an intense Jewish lifestyle for his family. He was the father of seven sons and two daughters, all of whom were grown up and married, and he had more than 30 grandchildren. Professionally he had done well in the family business and, together with his wife, he had built and supported two small Jewish high schools, one for boys and one for girls, and he had contributed to numerous other Jewish causes. In fact, it was thanks to his dedication and initiative that this particular community could thrive as it did.

At half past ten the lights flickered. As in most Orthodox households, the lights were on timers and regulated themselves automatically. One of the Ten Commandments forbids work on the Sabbath. Then many centuries ago the rabbis had named kindling a fire as one type of work. Turning electricity on and off, the modern equivalent, comes under this prohibition. It was time for bed, but the Sabbath was not over. The whole of the next day until after sunset would be dedicated to prayer, to fellowship, to the community, and to God. It was the Seventh Day of the week, the Sabbath, the day of rest, one of the great gifts of the Jewish people to the world.[1]

The Jewish Religious Establishment

This Sabbath scene is replicated in strictly Orthodox households in every big city in Europe and America and throughout the State of Israel. Other Jewish families celebrate the Sabbath in a different way. The less Orthodox may have a family meal which will involve saying the blessings and singing songs—but everyone, men, women, and children alike, will join in. In other families there is little obvious religious observance, but Friday evening and Saturday are still regarded as a special "home" time.

The strictly Orthodox are a small, but an immediately recognizable, group. The men wear their distinctive dress of dark suits, black hats, and ritual fringes. The women and girls follow rules of modesty. Skirts cover the knee; sleeves come over the elbow; necklines are high and stockings are always worn. Their lives are governed by the myriad provisions of *Torah* (Jewish law in the broadest sense). This means that they tend to live close together in self-defining comunities, because they need to be within walking distance of their synagogue. Almost all the men attend services daily, or even twice daily. There is strict separation between the men and the women in the synagogue building. Studying the law is largely the preserve of men while the women reign supreme in the home.

Except in cases of medical necessity, birth control is not encouraged. Young men and women marry young in their very early twenties, and a large family is regarded as a blessing. Even lovemaking is regulated by the *Torah*. During her monthly period and for seven days afterwards a woman is not permitted to have sexual relations with her husband. Every month, at the end of this time, the women bathe themselves in the community ritual bath (*mikveh*) and only then can marital relations be resumed. The children attend Jewish schools where boys and girls are taught separately and follow a different curriculum. In addition to their normal secular studies, they learn Hebrew and they study the Jewish sacred books. By the time they have reached their teens, the boys are reading the *Talmud*, the massive compendium of Jewish law compiled in Babylonia in the sixth century C.E. When they graduate from their Jewish high school, they do not go on to secular universities. Instead the boys attend a *Yeshiva* in which Jewish knowledge is the sole subject of study. The girls go to a seminary which has a modified curriculum and which will give them some sort of teaching certificate. During these years, under the careful supervision of their elders, the young people will meet, exchange views, become engaged, and marry. For the first few years of married life, it is quite usual for the couple to be supported by parents and relations. Only once *Talmudic* studies are finished and life-long habits established will the young man embark on the serious business of earning a living and providing for his family.

Despite its visibility, strict Orthodoxy is numerically a tiny movement. Of the six million Jews in the United States only three million identify with a synagogue, and of these only 300,000 are strict Orthodox. The majority of American Jews, therefore, do not regard themselves as Orthodox and most of those who do belong to what is called the **Modern Orthodox** (or sometimes Neo-Orthodox) movement. Adherents believe that it is possible to be an observant Jew, but, at the same time, to be fully conversant with modern culture. In their synagogues, the regular daily prayer services still take place and men and women sit separately. At the same time congregants wear more conventional formal dress. The majority of men, however, do wear their skull caps at all times (when awake and not bathing) and many Modern Orthodox do keep the Jewish food laws (the laws of *Kashrut*). Some compromise—perhaps keeping a *kosher* home, but eating anything when out. The children may attend Jewish schools, but they will be the kind of establishment in which secular subjects are every bit as important as Jewish Studies and the graduates expect to go on to conventional universities.

Unlike the strict Orthodox, who will have arranged marriages, the Modern Orthodox will choose their own marriage partners (hopefully within the community) and it is unusual for them to marry before the mid-twenties. There will not generally be an exceptionally large number of children and the wife will probably pursue her own profession.

Despite all these concessions to modernity, the Modern Orthodox movement continues to teach that the Jewish law, the Torah, is the inspired Word of God and that it was originally given to the Prophet Moses, when he stood before the Almighty on Mount Sinai (see page 77). As Samson Raphael Hirsch (1808–88), the founder of the movement, declared:

> If our religion so commanded us, we would abandon so-called civilization and progress. We would obey without question because we believe that our religion is the true religion. It is the word of God, and before it every other consideration must yield. The Jew has to judge everything by the unchangeable touchstone of his God given law. Anything which does not pass this test does not exist for him.[2]

Although the Orthodox control the religious establishment in the State of Israel and they are a powerful force in the United States and Europe, many Jews rejected what they saw as this fundamentalist understanding of Judaism. Instead, they set up alternate institutions and modes of worship, which in their opinion better expressed the essence of Judaism. In the nineteenth century, with the advent of Biblical criticism and with the increased opportunities available to Jews in the secular world, two important new movements arose. The **Reform** movement, which began in the early nineteenth century, encouraged religious diversity, free thinking and personal autonomy. Members of the Reform movement sought to stress what they saw as the more important ethical dimension of Judaism, over the merely ritualistic. In Orthodoxy, they argued, Judaism had become an inward-looking sect. But now, in an age of greater liberalism in Europe, it was time for universal Jewish values to be shared

more openly with Christian and even nonreligious fellow coun-
trymen. If that meant diluting the form of actual worship, as the
Orthodox accused them of doing, then so be it.

Reform Jews thus emphasized the importance of the
Prophetic tradition and correspondingly downplayed the *Talmudic* and rabbinic inheritance of the years of Jewish Exile. They
saw themselves as making Judaism more relevant to the modern
Jew, who now had at least one foot in general civil society. The
ethical precepts of the Ten Commandments, they said, should
take precedence over the minutiae of outdated laws concerning
animal sacrifice, ritually pure food, and other customs which
distinguished Jews from their non-Jewish fellows.

However, it was not long before the Reform movement itself
began subdividing, into those factions that favored moderate
change, and those that favored radical change—abandoning
Hebrew in favor of the local vernacular in synagogue services,
eliminating prayers which they thought overemphasized the
particularity of the Jewish people, even in some cases moving
the Sabbath from Saturday to Sunday, to be closer to their
Christian neighbors.

One of those new factions developed into **Conservative**
Judaism, an American movement which followed later in the
century, accepted that some changes were inevitable in the
modes of Jewish life and sought a compromise between Reform
and Orthodox. Today in the United States, the majority of those
who belong to a synagogue—about three million—choose to
join either a Conservative or a Reform congregation.

The Reform and the Conservative have important differences in belief and practice. As their names imply, the
Conservatives are more reluctant to depart from the age-old tradition than are the Reform. In other countries, like Great
Britain, France, and Hungary, simlar controversies developed
around nuances of worship, and created a plethora of new terms
for different sects. In Great Britain the more traditional
organization calls itself Reform, while the more radical
describes itself as Liberal. All these divisions share an accep-
tance of the findings of modern Biblical scholarship. Adherents

do not believe that the *Torah* was literally dictated by God to Moses. Instead they see it as a collection of traditions originating at different times in Ancient Israel. Certainly it was divinely inspired, but, at the same time, it was the product of developing human reflection.

This means that non-Orthodox Jews feel themselves entitled to adapt, or even to reject, certain provisions of Jewish law if they conflict with modern sensibility. Thus when the rabbis of the American Reform movement established their principles at a conference in Pittsburgh in 1885, they declared, "We accept as binding only the moral laws and maintain only such ceremonies as elevate and sanctify our lives, but we reject all such as are not adapted to the views and habits of modern civilization."[3] Since then the movement has grown and developed. Nonetheless, it is still true today that Reform Jews prefer to allow their members to obey or disobey the food laws as a matter of personal choice. They believe in the absolute equality of men and women and have rejected the laws of purity and divorce as being disadvantageous to women (see Chapter 5). Girls and boys receive exactly the same religious education and, in recent years, both the Conservative and the Reform movement have ordained women as rabbis.

In this century two other movements have come into being. **Reconstructionism** grew out of Conservative Judaism. Its founder Mordecai Kaplan (1881–1983) taught that Judaism should be understood as an evolving civilization that included both religious and secular elements. Belief in God was no longer necessary and synagogues should reconstruct themselves as centers for all aspects of Jewish culture. More radical still is **Humanistic Judaism**. This originated in Detroit, Michigan, under the leadership of Rabbi Sherwin Wine (b.-1928). He teaches that Judaism, like all other religions, is a purely human creation which is always changing; it embraces many beliefs and lifestyles and Wine extols the humanistic dimensions of the faith.

There is another factor to consider: many Jews have no religios affiliation whatsoever. About 50 percent do not belong to a synagogue; they do not send their children to religious school; many marry outside of the faith and freely enjoy all the advantages of a secular twentieth-century lifestyle.

Yet despite this apparent indifference to their religious heritage, many of these people still identify themselves as Jews and feel themselves to be Jewish. Some do this by getting involved in Jewish communal causes, like the campaign to help Soviet Jewry, giving to charities, or supporting educational institutions. Others affiliate with their Jewishness by learning the **Yiddish** of their forefathers, or listening to East European Jewish klezmer music. Yet others feel that by participating in general causes of social justice (like the Civil Rights movement, or gender equality) they are living out the ethical obligations of their Jewish heritage. One clear focus for this identification lies in their commitment to the Jewish State of Israel.

In such secular circles, it is commonplace to hear the justification, "We're not religious, but we do support Israel." The modern **Zionist** movement—which draws on the ancient Jewish belief in return to the land of Israel—was launched by the Austrian journalist Theodor Herzl (1869–1904) at the First Zionist Conference in 1897. Herzl believed that **anti-semitism** was endemic in European, Christian society and that Jews would never be safe as a minority group in a foreign land. In order to achieve freedom, they must have a land of their own. In its early days, Zionism was widely supported by the oppressed of Eastern Europe, but was largely rejected by the **Progressive** Jews of the prosperous New World. However, after the **Holocaust** of World War II (1931–45), when approximately one third of world Jewry was murdered in the Nazi death camps, public opinion changed. Today the whole Jewish community, Orthodox, Progressive, and secular, are united in their determination that the political State of Israel, which was created to provide a homeland for the Jews after the war, must survive.

The State of Israel

The establishment of the Jewish State in 1948 was seen by many as the fulfillment of a religious dream. Every year, at the spring festival of **Passover**, after the ritual meal has been eaten, the participants promise "Next Year in Jerusalem!" In this century, for the first time in nearly 2000 years since the end of Jewish sovereignty over Palestine in the first century C.E., this hope can become a reality.

Nazi anti-semitism and the Holocaust effectively destroyed the old Jewish communities of Eastern Europe. Those who survived the concentration camps all too often found that there was no place for them in their old homes. Israel became their goal and once the new State had come into existence, about two thirds of those Jews who had been languishing in the Displaced Persons' Camps settled there. The Israeli population has increased enormously. In 1946, there were approximately 600,000 Jews living in the land. By 1989, according to official calculations, the Jewish population was more than three and a half million. This increase took place in spite of the three devastating wars of 1956, 1967, and 1973, constant military danger, and almost insurmountable economic problems.

By no means all the immigrants were Holocaust survivors. Israel was in effect created by Jewish immigration, by a willingness to use weapons in self-defense, and by a resolution of the United Nations. The surrounding countries, Egypt, Jordan, Syria, and Lebanon, were implacably opposed to having a Jewish State in their midst. In consequence there was an enormous rise in Arab anti-semitism. The lives of Jews in many Islamic countries—who are known as **Sephardim** Jews—became intolerable and emigration to the **Promised Land** became an attractive proposition. There has been large-scale immigration from Turkey, Iraq, Syria, Lebanon, Iran, the Yemen, and the countries of North Africa. In addition the imagination of the world has been captured by the arrival of Black Jews from Ethiopia and by large numbers from the former Soviet Union, who are also fleeing from a long tradition of anti-semitism.

The State of Israel has also produced a few religious trends of its own. A former **Chief Rabbi** of Palestine, Rabbi Abraham Isaac Kook, attempted to explain the activities of atheist Zionist Jews in rebuilding the ancient Jewish state as something sacred, because it was, as he put it, part of the "Redemption of Israel." He also believed in *Torah im Derekh Eretz*—religion in the way of the land—a fusion of spiritual with practical values. In building bridges between secular and religious Jews, Kook gave new life to the religious Zionist trend known as the *Mizrakhi* movement. Thus today, most Modern Orthodox Jews in Israel seem to subscribe to *Mizrakhi* values.

Although there are Jews from many different countries in Israel and several internal religious movements, the electoral system of proportional representation has given the strictly Orthodox considerable influence there. The system enables them to retain their control over the rabbinical courts and to prevent the introduction of civil marriage and divorce. They receive financial support from the State for their own schools which concentrate on religious subjects. There are numerous *Yeshivot* and seminaries and, through the Ministry for Religious Affairs, synagogues and religious courts are funded by the government. There are two Chief Rabbis, who are state functionaries, one representing the **Ashkenazim** (Jews of Eastern European origin) and the other the *Sephardim* (Oriental Jews). The Ministry is controlled by the Orthodox and, despite the presence of progressive seminaries and synagogues, the non-Orthodox movements have a hard time. They receive no government money and are fiercely opposed by the religious establishment.

Many Israelis have little time for the traditional Jewish religion. The separation between the secular and the strictly Orthodox schools does little to help mutual understanding. The aggressive stance taken by some of the young strictly Orthodox on such matters as maintaining Sabbath observance (they have been known to throw stones at moving cars) and preventing archaeological digs (Jewish law forbids the exhumation of corpses) is understandably condemned by secular Israelis. The fact that the strictly Orthodox are exempted from military service on religious grounds means that they miss out on an important bonding experience. Even Orthodox Jews who *do* serve in the army occasionally present problems. Where their commitment to the *Torah* (as they see it) collides with their loyalty to the state, there can be terrible conflicts. The extreme example was the assassination of Prime Minister Yitzhak Rabin by an extremist *Yeshiva* student in November 1995, which outraged public opinion.

However, Israel remains a Jewish State and the focus of the Jewish world. Despite its many problems, social, military, economic, and religious, it inspires enormous loyalty. As the traditional Passover liturgy puts it, "This year we are here: next year we will be in the Land of Israel. This year we are slaves; next year we will be free..."[4]

Who is a Jew?

In one sense Judaism is fundamentally different from Christianity and Islam. Jewish identity does not depend primarily on accepting a belief system or on following a particular way of life. According to Jewish law, a person is Jewish if he or she has a Jewish mother. All those who can trace a straight **matrilineal** descent from someone who was accepted by the community as a Jewess are, by definition, Jewish themselves. According to the **Mishnah**, the anthology of Jewish law compiled in the second century C.E., "Thy son of an **Israelite** woman is called thy son, but thy son by a heathen woman is not called thy son."[5]

This definition had three notable advantages. First, it was clear and easy to understand. Secondly, the identity of a baby's mother is seldom a matter of debate since pregnancies and birth are almost invariably witnessed; paternity, on the other hand, is a far trickier matter. Thirdly, in the long history of abuse and persecution, any baby conceived as a result of rape could still be counted within the Jewish fold. Because Jewishness is a matter of physical descent, personal religious belief is irrelevant to status. It is quite possible to be a believing Muslim or Christian and still be a Jew, according to **halakhah**; history has produced many examples of such people. The *Torah* teaches that even apostates who have deliberately rejected the faith, remain Jews.

It is also possible to convert to Judaism. The *Talmud* describes the process:

> The rabbis say: Now if someone comes and wants to be a convert they say to him: Why do you want to be a convert? Don't you know that the Jews are harried, hounded, persecuted and harassed and that they suffer many troubles? If he replies: I know that and I am not worthy, then they receive him without further argument.[6]

In fact the process is generally more complicated than that. For many centuries, the Christian Church deemed it a capital offense to convert any Christian to Judaism. In addition the rabbis always taught that non-Jews were acceptable to God provided that they kept a few basic moral laws. Jews, on the other hand, have the obligation to follow the whole *Torah* in all its complexity. Therefore, they argued, there was no advantage to becoming a Jew and there was no point in encouraging converts.

The question of who is a Jew is complicated still further by a recent decision of the American Reform movement. It is a statistical fact that Jewish men are more likely to "marry out" than are Jewish women and the National Jewish Population Survey of 1990 showed that the total out-marriage rate was running at approximately 57 percent. In consequence the Reform Rabbinical association declared that the child of one Jewish parent (whether father or mother) is under the presumption of Jewish status and that the child of a Jewish father must be regarded as Jewish provided he or she had some form of regular Jewish education. This decision, of course, is unacceptable to the Orthodox and Conservatives who still adhere to the tradition of matrilineal descent.

The matter has come to a head with the existence of the State of Israel. Who is to be entitled to become an Israeli citizen? After much discussion, the **Knesset**, the Israeli elected assembly, passed the **Law of Return** which stated unequivocally that "Every Jew has the right to come to this country [Israel] as an immigrant." It went on to define "Jew" as a person who "was born of a Jewish mother or who had become converted to Judaism and is not a member of another religion." In addition, close family members of such people are also entitled to become Israeli citizens.[7] By refusing to define the nature of conversion to Judaism, all those who have come into the fold through the non-Orthodox movements are counted in. By allowing non-Jewish family members, Gentile spouses and children and many who cannot produce evidence of strict matrilineal descent can be included.

The Jewish Community in the World Today

The vast majority of the Jewish community has lived outside the Land of Israel for the last 2500 years. Before the start of World War II in 1939, it has been calculated that world Jewry numbered approximately 16.5 million. Of this, seven and a half million lived in Eastern Europe and Russia, two million in Western Europe, one million in Asia, half a million in Africa, and five and a half million in the New World.[8] Thus the largest Jewish community was that of Eastern Europe—in Poland, Austria-Hungary, the Balkans, Russia, and the Baltic States, where they constituted a prominent middle class in business and the professions. Here there was a flourishing religious life. Most Jews lived in **Shtetls,** small towns predominantly inhabited by Jews. The common language was Yiddish; young men studied *Talmud* in famous *Yeshivot*; traditional rituals were practiced in the home and life revolved around synagogue and home. A growing minority were making a new life for themselves in larger cities, like Warsaw in Poland, Vienna in Austria, and Odessa in southern Russia. The attractions of secular society led to increased **assimilation**. Many climbed the social rungs of their host society, becoming prominent lawyers, doctors, journalists, and so on. Yet their success also occasionally bred feelings of anti-semitism among non-Jewish fellow citizens, who resented their achievements.

The institutions of the *Shtetl* were slowly being eroded in the early twentieth century. Emigration to America offered new opportunities to these Eastern European Jews and it is estimated that between 1840 and 1925 more than two and a half million people of Jewish origin entered the United States as immigrants. The traditional way of life was finally destroyed in the catastrophe of the Nazi Holocaust. The figures tell a grim story. By 1948 world Jewry had been reduced to 11.5 million. Of these, nearly six million lived in the United States. The Jews of Western Europe now numbered only approximately one million; there were less than one million in Eastern Europe, nearly a further two million in the Soviet Union, and about half a million in the new State of Israel. Since then the population of Israel has substantially increased, but otherwise the new pattern was established. The United States remains the home of the biggest, richest, and most powerful Jewish community that the world has ever known. It is almost twice as large as that of the State of Israel, which comes second in size. Unlike the United States, where *Ashkenazi* Jews predominate, Israeli society is approximately half and half *Ashkenazi* and *Sephardi*. Third in line is that of the states of the former Soviet Union, but Jews there have been denied knowledge of their religious and cultural heritage during the years of the Communist regime.

So to see the fullness and diversity of Jewish life in the **Dispersion** (usually known by its Greek translation, Diaspora), it is necessary to look at the United States. The variety of institutions is bewildering. There are synagogues representing every shade of religious opinion, including prayer groups for those who are more comfortable in a feminist or in a homosexual ambience. Then there is the whole spectrum of Jewish charities. Jews are generous people and they support good causes liberally.

In every major American city there are Jewish old age homes and blocks of sheltered housing for the elderly and handicapped. There is a Jewish Family Agency, a Jewish hospital and a Jewish burial society. The community supports innumerable educational establishments, varying from strictly Orthodox *Yeshivot* to Progressive Jewish day schools, from synagogue nurseries to *kosher* summer camps. For young adults there are Jewish Community Centers offering a wide range of leisure activities, Jewish country clubs, libraries, museums, and extensive programs of adult education. Giving to Jewish charities is regarded as a **Mitzvah**, a good deed, and the Jewish institutions of the United States are very big business.

Not many families have been in the United States for more than three or four generations and, as in Israel, their forebears come from all over the world. The fourth largest community is that of France, which has approximately 600,000 Jews. This is a particularly interesting population in that it is a meeting of two distinct cultures. Although the old *Ashkenazi* community was decimated by the occupying Nazis during World War II, the survivors were joined by a large influx of *Sephardi* Jews from North Africa. Today more than half of all French Jews live in Paris, which has been described as "the largest and most lively centre of Jewish life in all Europe."[9]

Great Britain escaped Nazi domination in the War and its Jewish institutions survived intact. Today there are over 300,000 Jews in Britain, the majority of whom belong to the Orthodox United Synagogue under the leadership of the Chief Rabbi. However, although most identify as Orthodox, they do not necessarily follow an Orthodox lifestyle. Individual Jews have risen to powerful positions in the government, in commerce and industry, in the professions, and in the arts. There is little obvious evidence of anti-semitism and the population is well established. Indeed some families are descended from Jews who settled in the country as early as the seventeenth century.

There are still small communities in every country in Europe. In Asia outside Israel there are approximately half a million

Jews living as far apart as Turkey in the west and China in the east. A new synagogue has recently been built in Hong Kong. The Jews of India are a particularly fascinating group. They claim to have come to the country in Biblical times and there are several old communities, who seem to have had no contact with one another until the eighteenth century. In certain places, there is a caste system which distinguishes between White and Black Jews and, until recently, there was no inter-marriage between the subgroups.

In the New World outside the United States, there are more than 300,000 Jews living in Canada, nearly a quarter of a million in Argentina, and an equal number in the rest of Latin America. The community of South Africa numbers over 100,000 and there are more than 70,000 Jews in Australasia. All these populations have their own special characteristics. Some communities are ancient and some were created largely by refugees from Nazism.

North Africa has several ancient and important communities. In recent years, however, they have been greatly depleted. After Algeria became independent of French rule, the majority of Jews left, either for France or for Israel. Large-scale emigration has taken place from Tunisia and the important, historical community of Cairo: Egypt has been reduced to a few hundred Jews. Even in Morocco, where the King has frequently expressed his wish that his Jewish subjects live in peace and prosperity, the community has shrunk from over 200,000 to approximately 20,000.

However, the African group which has captured the newspaper headlines is that of Ethiopia. No one knows the true origin of the Jews of Ethiopia, but they themselves claim to be the descendants of King Solomon and the Queen of Sheba. There was some doubt as to their authenticity, but in 1973 the Israeli Chief Rabbinate pronounced them to be Israelites and two years later they were declared to be eligible for Israeli citizenship under the Law of Return.

Thus the Jewish community is essentially international. Many members have strong feelings of patriotism and identification with their native countries. At the same time, there is a sense of sharing a common history and experience. Jews are of all different races; they come from a wide variety of socioeconomic circumstances; they hold widely different beliefs. Yet, at the same time they are conscious of being a single people and the idea of *K'lal Israel* (the whole of Israel) is very important to them, even if they disagree on what that means.

Judaism in Biblical Times

The early history of the Israelites—ancestors of the Jewish people—is based largely on the stories recounted in the Hebrew Bible. Jews also know this book as the *Tanakh* (a Hebrew acronym for its three component parts); while Christians call it the Old Testament, and incorporate it into their scriptures. The

 first five books of the Bible are known as the **Pentateuch** (*Torah*), and it is in the first book, Genesis, that the essentials of the Jewish faith—God's creation of the world—are explained.

Scholars are uncertain, however, of the historical accuracy of these Biblical accounts because some of the events, people, and genealogies included can not be supported by archaeological findings or by references to the Israelites in the writings of peoples in neighboring lands.

Jews believe themselves to be descended from the **Patriarch** Abraham who Biblical narratives and genealogies suggest lived somtime between 1700–1900 B.C.E. Abraham was a native of the Middle Eastern city of Ur (in present-day Iraq). God promised that if he left his comfortable life, he would become the father of a great nation. Even though he and his wife were not young and they had no children, Abraham accepted the call and became a nomadic herdsman. In the course of time, he had a son, Ishmael (c.1850 B.C.E.) by a slave woman, who was to become the father of the Arab peoples. But Ishmael was not to be the heir of God's promise. Finally, against all expectation, Abraham's elderly wife, Sarah, produced her own son, Isaac (c.1850 B.C.E.). A **Covenant** relationship was established between God and the Patriarch. God promised that he would protect and preserve Abraham's family, they would be as numerous as the stars of heaven, and they would be His **Chosen People**. On their part, Abraham's descendants must obey God's commandments. As a symbol of the covenant, the practice of circumcision was instituted: "Every male among you shall be circumcised... It will be a sign of the covenant between you and me... He that is eight days old among you shall be circumcised."[1] To this day, many secular Jews have their sons circumcised. It remains a basic article of faith.

The three Patriarchs, Abraham, his son Isaac, and his grandson Jacob (c.1750 B.C.E.), are all revered in the Jewish tradition. Jacob was also given the name of Israel ("One who has striven with God"). Later, Jacob took his entire family and settled in Egypt. He was the father of twelve sons who, in their turn, were the fathers of the Twelve Tribes of the Jewish people. Initially they had been privileged immigrants, but the Book of Exodus describes how "There arose a new king over Egypt who did not know Joseph [Jacob's second youngest son]."[2] The Egyptians enslaved the Israelites and set them to building cities. However, a young Jew named Moses, who, according to the story, had been brought up at the pharaoh's court, was inspired by God to lead his people to freedom. God sent a series of ten plagues upon the land. The last one was the death of all the firstborn. The Israelites avoided this calamity. They were instructed to kill a lamb and smear its blood on the door posts of their houses. On seeing the stain, the Angel of Death would "pass over" the house. So great was the horror that the Egyptians finally allowed the Jews to leave. They gathered their possessions together, not even giving themselves time for their bread to rise, and they fled the country. This event is still celebrated by Jews today as Passover (**Pesach**), one of the most important festivals of the faith. It is a celebration of freedom. For eight days, nothing made with a raising agent is eaten and the festival begins with a family dinner at which the story of their ancestors' escape from slavery in Egypt is told again.

For 40 years, the fugitives wandered in the desert of the Sinai peninsula. It was during this time that Moses received the ultimate revelation. On Mount Sinai, he was given the *Torah*, the Jewish law. This is enshrined in the Pentateuch, the first five books of the Jewish Scriptures, the books of Genesis, Exodus, Leviticus, Numbers, and Deuteronomy. The Orthodox believe that the *Torah* was literally dictated by God to Moses. As Maimonides (1135–1204), the great philosopher and codifier, put it: "I believe with perfect faith that the whole and complete Law as we know it is one and the same as that given to Moses... I believe with perfect faith that the Law will never be changed, nor that any other law will be given in its place by the Creator."[3] Reform and Conservative Jews adopt what they see as a more flexible position, but for all Jews, the *Torah* is the foundation of their religious life. Every week in the synagogue, the pious read from the *Torah* **Scroll**, and the cycle of the Pentateuch is completed every year. In a very real sense, the Jews are a people of the book.

The Book of Joshua describes the Israelite conquest of Canaan (modern day Israel), which was seen as God's Promised Land. Initially the Israelites were led by a series of charismatic judges who arose at times of military danger, but gradually the need for a king was felt. The Twelve Tribes first chose a young man named Saul (eleventh century B.C.E.), but he committed suicide after a devastating defeat inflicted by a neighboring nation. He was succeeded by David (tenth century B.C.E.) who, in the tradition, is regarded as in many ways the ideal king. He conquered the city of Jerusalem and made it his capital, and God promised that He would establish his descendants "for ever and hold your throne for all generations."[4] Jews still believe that when God sends a new king, a **Messiah** (the anointed one), to bring about divine rule on earth, the chosen one will be descended from David.

David's son, King Solomon (d.c. 930 B.C.E.) built the magnificent **Temple** in Jerusalem. It was dedicated to the One God

The exodus of the Israelites from Egypt—celebrated during the festival of Passover (Pesach)—is a central event in the history of the Jewish people. Under the leadership of Moses, the Israelites were delivered from bondage and escaped from their pursuers on dry land when the Red Sea miraculously parted.

and here sacrifices were offered daily in praise of the Almighty and in atonement for Israel's sins. However, after the death of Solomon, the Ten Northern Tribes split away from the Two Southern and established their own kingdom. During the period of the Divided Kingdoms (930–722 B.C.E.) many of the Biblical **Prophets** were at work. Elijah (ninth century B.C.E.), Hosea, Amos, Micah, and Isaiah (all eighth century B.C.E.) warned the people of impending disaster. They were convinced that God would punish His people because they ignored His word, led wicked lives, and were not faithful to the Covenant. So powerful was Elijah in particular that he did not die, but was taken up to Heaven in a fiery chariot. It is still believed by the Orthodox that he is waiting to return to herald the days of the Messiah.

The prophecies proved to be all too accurate. In 721 B.C.E., the Assyrians (from modern day Iraq) destroyed the Northern Kingdom. The Ten Northern Tribes disappeared from history. Although legend maintained that they still survived in some far-away region and could yet be gathered together in the days of the messiah, the reality is that they intermarried with neighboring tribes and lost their national and religious identity. Then in 586 B.C.E. the Babylonians, the successors of the Assyrians, conquered the Two Southern Tribes (Judah and Benjamin). They destroyed King Solomon's Temple in Jerusalem and they took the Jews into exile. It was a devastating experience. Nonetheless, sustained partly by the words of the Biblical Prophets and by the Law, the Jews survived. The Prophet Ezekiel comforted the people by reminding them of God's faithfulness: "I will rescue them from all places where they have been scattered on a day of cloud and thick darkness. And I will bring them out from the peoples, and gather them from the countries and will bring them into their own land."[5]

During the long years of exile from the Promised Land, the Jewish leaders built up a hope for the future. They looked for a kingly figure, a messiah, who would restore the nation to its former glory and put an end to all human conflict. More importantly, this period marked the flowering of the prophetic tradition. Not only did the Prophets condemn Jews for adopting pagan practices, they also chided the people of Israel for their past misdeeds, and insisted that they return to the true spirit of the law, and not just empty rituals. The Prophets did not want Jews to ignore the rituals but sought to remind them of ethical obligations. Scholars see this as a deepening sophistication in Judaism, even a movement away from particularist features to a new universalism. At the same time, the Prophets also warned of the dangers to Jewish identity in a political arena full of enemies.

The Jewish leaders also seem to have developed the practice of meeting together on a regular basis. They could no longer offer sacrifices because the Temple was the only proper place for that, but they could come together to pray and to study the *Torah*. This was the start of the synagogue as an institution. Less than 70 years later, the Babylonians, in their turn, were conquered by the Persians (from modern-day Iran). Although many chose to remain where they were in the comforts of Babylon, a group of the faithful struggled back to the Promised Land. Under the leadership of Zerubbabel (a descendant of David) and the priest Haggai, they rebuilt the Temple. It was on a far smaller scale than the previous building, but sacrifice could be resumed. However, from that time on, there were two centers of world Jewry, Judaea (the old Southern Kingdom) centered on Jerusalem and the Dispersion, with its center in Babylonia.

Things were not easy for the returned exiles, but the situation was transformed by Nehemiah (fifth century B.C.E.) who was appointed governor of the land in 445 B.C.E. The scribe Ezra (fifth century B.C.E.) gathered the people together and read the Law to them. The listeners were transfixed. They were immediately determined to keep the festivals prescribed in the *Torah*: *Pesach* (Passover), **Shavuot** (weeks) and **Sukkot** (**tabernacles**). These were agricultural celebrations as well as commemorations of God's goodness in liberating the Jews from slavery, giving Moses the Law, and preserving the Israelites in the wilderness. In addition, Ezra insisted that the people divorce their foreign wives so that the land would be purged of idolatrous influences. Even today, the Jews see their faithfulness to the *Torah* and their aversion to **intermarriage** as the cornerstones of their ethnic and religious survival as a people.

The Second Temple and the Dispersion

The Babylonians had not taken the entire Jewish population into Babylon, only the leaders and the affluent and influential. The "people of the land" had been left behind. They intermarried with people of other settled populations, but they retained their belief in the One God. When the exiles returned, these people had been eager to stress their relationship with the Jews and had offered to help rebuild the Temple. The Jews did not want their assistance. Once the **Samaritans**, as they came to be called, saw that they were not to be accepted as Israelites, they developed their own, separate, traditions. A small group survives to this day. They insist that their version of the *Torah* is the correct one and that their **High Priest** is descended from the family of Moses' brother Aaron, the first Hight Priest. In 333 B.C.E. they were given permission to build their own Temple on Mount Gerizim. They claim that this is the only place where it is permissible to offer sacrifice and that it was chosen by God. This Temple was destroyed by Jewish forces in around 128 B.C.E., but the Samaritans continue to offer the Passover sacrifice on their mountain and to practice their ancient form of Israelite religion.

Judaea itself continued to be occupied by foreign powers. In 333 B.C.E., the King of Persia was defeated by Alexander the Great (352–323 B.C.E.) of Macedonia (Northern Greece). Alexander's aim was to spread Greek culture throughout the world. He conquered a huge empire which extended from Greece to the borders of India and included Egypt and Babylonia. When he died of fever, his lands were divided between many generals. After 20 years of fighting the number of generals was reduced to three. Ptolemy I founded the Ptolemaic dynasty in Egypt, Seleucus I the Seleucid dynasty in Mesopotamia, and Antigonus I the Antigonid dynasty in Asia

Minor and Macedonia. Initially, Judaea was under the control of the Ptolemies of Egypt. In general, the Ptolemies were tolerant of Jewish religious practice and there was a thriving Jewish community in the city of Alexandria on the Nile delta. Although these Egyptian Jews remained faithful to the God of their ancestors, they spoke Greek and enjoyed a fairly assimilated lifestyle. The Hebrew Scriptures were first rendered into Greek in Alexandria; the translation was known as the **Septuagint**. Alexandria was also the home of the eminent Jewish philosopher, Philo (c. 25 B.C.E.–40 C.E.) who tried to integrate Greek philosophy and Jewish religious teaching into a unified whole.

By 198 B.C.E. a Seleucid king, Antiochus III (reigned 223–187 B.C.E.), had taken over the control of Judaea. Although he did share the tolerant attitude of his predecessors, he was determined to turn Jerusalem into a Greek city. Various measures were introduced such as Greek games in which the athletes competed naked. This was totally abhorrent to the Jewish tradition. The next monarch, Antiochus IV (reigned 175–163 B.C.E.) was even more insensitive. He occupied the city, banned circumcision, and plundered the Temple treasures. He rededicated the building to Zeus, the king of the Greek gods, and he ordered that the sacrifices should include pigs, which the Jews regard as ritually unclean (or unkosher). Conflict arose between those Jews who wished to liberalize Jewish practice in the interest of greater assimilation with the Greek world, and the Jewish traditionalists led by the priest Mattathias (d.c.167 B.C.E.) and then by his sons, particularly Judas (known as *Maccabee*, the hammer, d.c.160 B.C.E.). Antiochus' army supported the **Hellenizers** but the traditionalists succeeded in recapturing Jerusalem. Their first priority was to cleanse the Temple and to rededicate it to God. Supposedly there was only enough holy oil to sustain the great light for one day, but miraculously it lasted for eight. These events are commemorated at the winter festival of lights (*Hanukkah*). Today the community lights candles for eight days to celebrate this victory of the Jews over foreign influences.

ART FOCUS
Jewish Art

THE SECOND OF THE TEN COMMANDMENTS reads, "You shall not make for yourself a graven image, or any likeness of anything that is in Heaven above, or that is in the earth beneath…" (Exodus 20:4). This has largely been understood as a prohibition against any form of idolatry (excessive worship of images) and the making of any image of God. While Jews have been less strict than Muslims in their rejection of all pictorial art, there has been a general reluctance to reproduce the human figure or face in a religious context.

However, there is a strong craft tradition among the Jews. In many places, particularly in Islamic lands, Jews have been famous as metal workers and much care has been lavished on the production of ritual objects. Every Jewish home should have a *mezuzah* on the door (a small box containing a prescribed portion of Scripture). This may be made of silver, wood, glass, or plastic and an enormous variety of design exists. Similarly, most families possess a wine cup and a set of candlesticks; both necessary for the celebration of the Sabbath and other festivals. Again, there is no uniform design and they can be made of a variety of materials. Often they are objects of real beauty.

In the synagogue itself, it is customary to keep the Scrolls of the Law either in a metal case or in a cloth cover. Both may be richly decorated. Attached to the wooden Scrolls there may be elaborate metal finials (ornaments). These are often hung with bells, reminiscent of the priests' vestments in the Temple in Jerusalem. Alternatively they may be hung with crowns, symbolising the fact that the *Torah*, the law, is the ruler of Jewish life. Over the cover is hung a silver breast-plate or shield, sometimes engraved with the Ten Commandments, but invariably a splendid example of the silvermaker's art. Because the Scroll itself is regarded as sacred, the text is not touched by the human hand. Instead a pointer is used. This is often made of silver and is frequently fashioned in the shape of a pointing human hand.

Most characteristic of all is the seven-branched candlestick. This was part of the furnishings of the Temple in Jerusalem. As the relief on the Arch of Titus shows (see page 46), it was carried in triumph to Rome when the Temple was sacked in 70 C.E. It has remained a prominent symbol of Judaism and has appeared in many forms and been understood in different ways throughout the history of Judaism.

Ancient Jewish catacomb on the Appian Way, Rome. The practice of burying the dead in subterranean tunnels, with side recesses for tombs, originated with the Jews of Palestine.

Mattathias's descendants succeeded in founding a dynasty of both rulers and High Priests. The Seleucid kings were compelled to acknowledge the independence of Judaea and the kingdom was extended to include Idumea, Galilee, and northern Trans-Jordan. The inhabitants of all these areas were compelled to convert to Judaism. But the Jewish empire was not to survive. By the middle of the first century B.C.E., the Romans had annexed Judaea and had turned it into a client state. Herod (73–4 B.C.E.), the son of an Idumean military governor of Judaea under the Romans, was an official in Galilee. When the Romans were expelled by the Parthians, Herod fled but returned with a Roman army in 37 B.C.E. to reconquer Judaea. He was then made King of Judaea by the Romans and he ruled until his death. Despite being a Jew by religion, he was detested by his people as a usurper. Nonetheless, he did a great deal for the country. He built the new port of Caesarea (named for his Roman master); he negotiated various privileges for the Jews of the Roman Empire; and he rebuilt the Temple on a splendid scale. It was magnificent. It contained an outer court where everyone, Jew and non-Jew, could mingle, another court for Jewish women, a further court for male Israelites, and a court of priests where the hierarchy offered the daily sacrifices. The innermost sanctuary was the **Holy of Holies**. This was hidden from sight by a curtain and it was only entered once a year by the High Priest on the **Day of Atonement** (*Yom Kippur*). There he would beg God's forgiveness on his people. Today the Day of Atonement with its preceding **Ten Days of Penitence** remains the most solemn season of the Jewish year.

The Temple was administered by the hereditary priests. They were said to have been descended from Moses' brother Aaron, to whom it was said "the priesthood shall be theirs by a perpetual statute."[6] They were drawn from a group known as the **Sadducees**, who were possibly named for Zadok (tenth century B.C.E.), the High Priest of King Solomon who had also served under King David. They are mentioned in the **New Testament** and are described by the historian Josephus (c. 38–c. 100 C.E.). They upheld the complete authority of the Pentateuch and they rejected the permanent validity of a body of oral interpretations of the law. As a result, they did not believe in such doctrines as the **Resurrection** of the dead since these developed as a result of discussing the complicated implications of the Biblical text. They were not a large group, but, as the aristocrats of the Jewish nation, they exerted a great deal of influence and as the group most in authority had to deal with the Romans. The **Pharisees** were quite different. They were described as scribes and sages and they were famous for their verbal interpretations of the sacred books. Regularly in the synagogues they expounded the deeper meanings of the Scriptures and, as the self-appointed moral leaders of the people, they devised a complex body of **Oral Law** over the years. By the first century B.C.E., every Judaean village contained a synagogue where the people could gather together and listen to the Pharisees' sermons.

There were other sects in Judaea at the time. The **Essenes** were a monastic group who led ascetic lives while they waited for God's salvation. We know about them from Josephus and also because they were probably the original owners of the famous **Dead Sea Scrolls**. The **Zealots** were freedom fighters and political guerrillas. After the death of Herod in 4 B.C.E., Judaea was subject to a series of rulers and Roman governors. It was not a happy time. There was hostility between the rich and the poor, a series of famines, and an increased sense of messianic excitement. One sect in particular, the followers of Jesus of Nazareth, was particularly imbued with this fervor. They claimed that the Kingdom of Heaven was dawning. After the crucifixion of Jesus, they hailed their martyred leader as the promised Messiah, believed in his resurrection, and in time broke away from other Jews to become a distinct and separate religion, Christianity. These events are described in the Christian New Testament, or the **Gospels**, and today Christianity is the world's largest religion.

Matters came to a head in 66 C.E. The Zealots raised a revolt and took control of the city of Jerusalem. The Roman armies marched in from the north and laid siege to the city. By late summer 70 C.E the daily sacrifices were suspended, and on

The Arch of Titus was erected in 81 C.E. by the Roman senate in honor of Vespasian and Titus. It commemorates the Roman victory over the Jews in the war of 66–70 C.E.

August 24 the beautiful Temple of Herod went up in flames. After the devastation, all that remained standing was the extreme Western **Wall**. This remains the most sacred place in the Jewish world and is a goal of pilgrimage. Even secular Jews return to the land of their forefathers to say their prayers or just to stand in awe in front of the great Wall. Meanwhile the Zealots continued to hold out in the south, at the fortress of Masada. When the rebellion was finally subdued, the Romans held a triumphal procession through the streets of Rome displaying the spoils of the Temple. This is recorded on the Arch of Titus which still stands in the Roman *forum* (marketplace).

There was a further Jewish rebellion against Rome in 132 C.E., but this had been put down by 135 C.E. Around this time the Roman emperor Hadrian converted Jerusalem into a pagan city, and forbade Jews from living there. He also renamed the province of Judaea as *Palestina*—Palestine—after the Jews' old enemy, the Philistines—a deliberate attempt to obliterate the connection between the land and the Jewish people. Scholars regard this as the definitive end of Jewish political sovereignty in their Promised Land, at least for the next 1800 years or so. The Jews had to come to terms with a new religious system which could no longer be centered on the Temple, the priesthood, and sacrifice. By this stage there were Jewish colonies in all the major urban centers around the Mediterranean Sea. Increasingly the Jewish religious establishment was to concentrate on the needs and developments of these growing Dispersion communities.

Rabbinic Judaism

With the Temple a charred ruin, Judaism could have disappeared like so many of the cults of the ancient world. Its survival was largely due to the vision and dedication of the Pharisees. During the siege of Jerusalem, Rabbi Johanan ben Zakkai (first century C.E.) escaped from the city and founded an academy on the coast at Javneh. There groups of scholars gathered to discuss, develop, and preserve the legal tradition. Under Johanan's successor, Gamaliel II (early second century C.E.), the supreme legal body of the Jews, the **Sanhedrin**, was reestablished and the learned came from far and near to listen to and participate in the debates. The **canon** of Scripture was decided, regular daily prayers were organized, and a system of rabbinical ordination for Jewish leaders was established.

Activities were only temporarily halted by the rebellion of 132–5 C.E., although the Javneh academy was transferred to Galilee. By the second century C.E., the oral interpretations of the law had become highly complex and Judah ha-**Nasi** (the patriarch) set himself the task of recording the debates and decisions on each particular topic. His official position and authority allowed his book of legal opinions, the *Mishnah*, to become the officially accepted one. The text of this great law book is divided into six orders: *Zeraim* dealing with the laws of agriculture, *Moed* with the laws of Sabbaths, fasts and festivals, *Nashim* with the laws of marriage and divorce, *Nezikin* with the civil and criminal law, *Kodashin* with the laws of Temple ritual and sacrifice, and *Tohorot* with the laws of ritual purity. It is not merely a summary of conclusions. The debates are recorded with the minority view expressed first ("Rabbi Simeon says... ") and each account ends with the final conclusion ("But the sages declare... "). It is an astonishing piece of work and by accomplishing it, Judah ha-Nasi provided a solid foundation upon which further discussion could be based.

At that time the Jewish leaders were also preoccupied with the correct interpretation of the Scriptures. The rabbinic interpretation of Holy Writ is known as **Midrash**. Since the Pentateuch, in particular, is regarded as the Word of God, it is vital that it should be correctly understood. Various experts devised rules for **exegesis** so that conflict could be avoided. For example, the fourth of the Ten Commandments reads: "Remember the Sabbath day and keep it holy. Six days shall you labor and do your work, but the seventh day is a Sabbath to the Lord your God."[7] By following the rules, the rabbis decided that there were 39 different types of work to be avoided. These include harvesting and kindling a fire, which is why Orthodox Jews today will neither pick a flower nor turn on an electric light during the Sabbath.

Meanwhile, other scholars founded centers elsewhere. In Galilee there were well-known academies in Tiberias, Caesarea, and Sepphoris. The Jewish community of Babylonia was not to be left behind. There the King recognized the community leader and gave him the title of **Exilarch**. This was an hereditary office and its holders claimed to be related to King Jehoiachin (sixth century B.C.E.), the last Judaean king of Davidic descent.

At the same time famous schools of learning were established at Sura in Central Mesopotamia and Pumbedita on the river Euphrates. The heads of these academies held the title of **Gaon**. Together with the Exilarch, the *Geonim* controlled the powerful Babylonian community. There scholars were not known as rabbi; this was a title only bestowed by the laying on of hands at ordination and it only applied in Judaea. Babylonian authorities were known as **Rav**. It should be pointed out that the modern title of rabbi is used somewhat differently. Today a rabbi is one learned in Jewish law, who has been ordained to teach and preach and who generally serves a congregation full time. The Judaean and Babylonian scholars almost invariably had secular occupations from which they gained their livelihood. Only in the Middle Ages did the title "rabbi" come to mean the spiritual leader of a particular Jewish community.

The work of interpreting the law continued. By the end of the fourth century C.E., the rabbis of Judaea had assembled the teachings of further generations of scholars on four of the six orders of the *Mishnah*. The additional material was described as *Gemara* (completion) and the whole is known as the Palestinian (or Jerusalem) *Talmud*. The same work was being accomplished in Babylonia. The Babylonian *Talmud* was completed in the sixth century C.E. It is nearly four times as long as its Palestinian counterpart and is considered to be more authoritative because of the lasting influence of the Babylonion schools and Exilarchate well into the Muslim period. It is quite extraordinary. Not only does it record the legal judgments and debates, it contains information on medicine, history, science, and agriculture. There are proverbs and fairy tales, folk legends, and rules of etiquette. It has been compared with a great sea with its constant free association of ideas. Throughout the Middle Ages, it was the main study of the Babylonian academies and it spread throughout the Jewish world. To this day it remains the main text in the Orthodox *Yeshivot* and many enjoy dipping into its riches. Even though many of its provisions are no longer relevant—such as those pertaining to the Temple and Priesthood— they are still read. Within the Orthodox community today, *Talmudic* study remains a lifetime commitment.

However, not all Jews regarded this development of the Oral Law with favor. In the days of the Temple, the aristocratic Sadducees believed that only the **Written Law** was authoritative and that later oral interpretation could be ignored. It seems that despite the efforts of the Palestinian and Babylonian sages, this strand of opinion survived within the community. In c. 760 C.E. Anan ben David, who had been passed over for the Exilarchate, set up his own alternative movement. Anan's principle was "Search thoroughly in the *Torah* and do not rely on my opinion." He insisted that the whole law was to be found in the Scriptures and not in rabbinical interpretation. Gradually the movement spread. Adherents were known as the **Karaites** and by the tenth century, communities were established in Egypt, North Africa, Persia, Babylonia, and Palestine. The rabbis resisted this incursion, but failed to stamp it out. Many eminent Biblical scholars of the early Middle Ages were of Karaite origin and they were as persecuted as their **Rabbanite** co-religionists in the Christian **crusades**, which sought to evict the Muslims from Palestine. By the sixteenth century, however, their numbers were in decline and by the mid twentieth century communities survived only in the Crimea, Egypt, and a few in Eastern Europe. The creation of the State of Israel in 1948 made a difference. They were regarded as eligible for immigration under the Law of Return and many took advantage of this. Today there is a community of approximately 7000 Karaites living in Israel. They maintain their own customs, have their own ritual butchers, and support their own religious court. But both by the laws of Israel, and by their own custom, they are not allowed to intermarry with the Israeli population.

The Growth and Challenge of Christianity

Today there are Jews living all over the world. We know that by the first century C.E. there were communities in all the major cities of the Mediterranean. The Christian missionary Paul (first century C.E.) wrote of his plans to visit Spain in his Epistle to the Romans,[8] and since he always preached first to the Jews, we must presume that there were Jewish colonies in the west. In the early days, Judaism itself seems to have been a missionary religion. In the New Testament, Jesus described the Pharisees crossing "land and sea to make a single **proselyte** [convert]."[9] All this changed in the fourth century once Christianity had become the official religion of the Roman Empire. Christians felt that their New Testament added to and "completed" the Old Testament. As Christian theology developed, it emphasized that by accepting the Kingship of Jesus, Christians, and no longer the Jews, were the elected nation of God. In addition the conversion of Gentiles to the new faith, and the adoption of Hellenistic ideas, made the rift between them and their Jewish antecedents irreparable.

The early Christians believed that they were the true inheritors of the privileges of Israel and that the Jews were hard-hearted and blind in their rejection of their own Messiah. By the time the Gospels were written, the Jews were perceived as demonic. For polemical reasons, the New Testament writers interpolated conflicts between Jesus and the Jewish leaders into their narratives. Blame for the death of Jesus was placed squarely on the Jews—"His blood be on us and on our children"[10]—and the seeds were sown for nearly 20 centuries of Christian anti-semitism.

In Christian Europe, the Jewish communities were self-contained units. The Christian rulers allowed each area to establish its own rules and by the tenth century there were important centers of Jewish learning in Northern France and in the Rhinelands. Jews had settled in England at the time of the Norman conquest in 1066 and there were small communities throughout France, and the Holy Roman Empire (present-day Netherlands, Germany, and Austria). Important scholars included the great Biblical commentator Rashi (Solomon ben Isaac of Troyes, 1040–1105), whose work on the Scriptures and the *Talmud* are still standard texts today. Yet Jewish existence in Christian Europe was never secure. The Church continued to teach that it was the Jewish people alone who were responsible for the death of the Christian Messiah, Jesus, and there were periodic outbreaks of violence against the community.

The situation was made worse by the crusades. By the eleventh century, the Muslim Turks were in control of the Holy

Land and the Christian holy places. The princes of Europe were encouraged by the Church to send armies to fight the Infidel. If it was meritorious to slaughter Muslims abroad, then it seemed only logical to harass the Jews at home, because both were considered infidels. Then, when the Black Death raged through the continent in the fourteenth century, the Jews were widely accused of causing the disease by poisoning the wells. Terrible accusations were made against them.

As early as 1144, the community of Norwich, England, was charged with using the blood of Christian children in the manufacture of Passover unleavened bread. The **Blood Libel**, as it was called, spread throughout Europe. The entire community was expelled from England in 1290; a few years later the French King evicted all the Jews from the French crown lands. In 1298 Christian mobs destroyed approximately 150 Jewish settlements in Germany. Then, in 1492, after the Christian monarchs Ferdinand and Isabella had driven out the Muslim rulers from Spain, they also exiled the ancient and successful Jewish community from their dominions.

This made the hospitality of Poland seem very attractive. Here from the thirteenth century, the Jews were protected. They were used by the great Polish nobles to collect taxes and manage the huge estates. The religious wars of the Protestant Reformation and Catholic Counter-Reformation in the sixteenth century also led to the migration of Jews from central to Eastern Europe. By the end of the sixteenth century the Jewish communities of Poland and the Baltic States were the largest and most powerful in Europe. They benefited from a system of communal autonomy. **Yiddish** (a German and Hebrew language written in Hebrew characters) was the common language and the rabbis ran their own religious courts and *Yeshivot.*

Meanwhile the Jews had fared differently in the Muslim countries. The founder of Islam in southern Arabia, Muhammed (c. 590–632), had hoped that the Jews would accept his message. Like them, he taught that God is One, and he adopted certain Jewish rituals such as a **fast** day, similar to the Day of Atonement. Like the Jews, the Muslims may not eat pork, they have fixed times for prayer, and they reject the worship of images. Much of Muhammed's original legislation was similar to the Jewish *halakhah* (law) and, like the Jews, the Muslims have an extensive tradition of Oral Law. Nonetheless, the Jews of Arabia were not prepared to acknowledge that Muhammed was God's Prophet, and in consequence Muhammed became hostile to them. In particular, the Jewish community of Medina was expelled and destroyed.

Despite this unfortunate beginning, Muslim rulers have generally been tolerant toward the Jews and have seen their value. Since they were **monotheists** (believers in one God), they were not regarded as infidels and there was no obligation to fight a holy war against them. Although there were negative incidents, generally the Jews were allowed to live in Muslim territory and enjoy religious freedom. In return they were expected to wear distinctive clothing which marked them out as Jews, they were not allowed to make converts, and they were obliged to pay an additional annual poll tax. This, of course, had the effect of maintaining their distinctive identity. There were many successful communities living in Muslim lands throughout the Middle Ages.

In the Iberian peninsula there were poets such as Judah Halevi (1075–1141), Moses ibn Ezra (c.1055–c.1135), and Solomon ibn Gabirol (c.1021–c.1056), and philosophers such as Bahya ben Joseph ibn Pakuda (c.1050–1120), Abraham ben David Halevi ibn Daud (c.1110–80), and Hasdai Crescas (1340–1412). Most famous of all was Maimonides (Moses ben Maimon, 1135–1204). He not only produced a comprehensive codification of the corpus of the Jewish law (the *Mishneh Torah*), but his philosophical work, *The Guide to the Perplexed*, set the tone for all subsequent debate. However, the glory of Spanish Jewry was not to last. After Spain was conquered by the Christians, there was a period of uncertainty. Then in 1492 all the Jews were expelled from Spanish soil. The only reprieve was baptism. The members of this rich, cultured, and successful community were scattered. Some went to North Africa, some to Italy, some to Holland, and others to Turkey.

The *Sephardim* and *Ashkenazim*

By this time, it was clear that two different traditions were exist-
ing side by side. Jews who traced their descent from ancestors
who had settled in Christian Europe in the Middle Ages were
known as the *Ashkenazim* ("German"). They lived in the
German States and, after the persecutions, in Austria, Poland,
the Baltic States, and Russia. Meanwhile, those who were
descended from the Jews of Spain, North Africa, and Babylonia
were known as the *Sephardim* ("Oriental"). Each group fully
recognized the other's Jewishness, but they used different liturgical rites and had many different customs. There were local differences even within the broader *Ashkenazi* and *Sephardi* communities. The *Ashkenazim* composed hymns, known as
Piyyutim, and penitential prayers (**Selihot**). They were known
for their piety, their strict adherence to Jewish law, and their
Talmudic scholarship. The *Sephardim*, on the other hand, were
thought to be more open to secular culture and were known for
their legal codes and their liturgical creativity. This may have
been because their host culture was more open to participation
of the *Sephardim* in their culture. The difference is well illustrated by the seventeenth-century communities of the Dutch
city of Amsterdam. The original community was *Ashkenazi*, but,
after the great expulsion, many Spanish Jews settled there.
Contemporary engravings of the Spanish and German synagogues show the Spanish congregation as far more affluent,
genteel, and worldly; indeed the worshipers look as if they are
dressed for a gala theatrical performance. The German synagogue was darker and smaller; the women were banished to a
remote balcony and there was an atmosphere of intense piety.
The differences in custom were openly acknowledged. When the
Sephardic legal authority Joseph Caro (1488–1575) published
his great code of Jewish law, the *Shulhan Arukh* ("Prepared
Table"), Moses Isserles (1525–72) had to add a supplement to
make it acceptable to the Ashkenazim. Having said that, it is
remarkable how consistent the essential Jewish laws were in the
two communities.

The population of the modern State of Israel is a mixture of *Sephardim* and *Ashkenazim*. When the State was founded in 1948, it was seen primarily as a refuge for the survivors of the Nazi Holocaust—the *Ashkenazim*. In fact, many of the *Sephardim* communities living in Arab-ruled countries were then so harassed by their rulers that they took the opportunity to immigrate.

The *Hasidim* and *Mitnagdim*

By the start of the modern period, Jews were established throughout Europe, North Africa, and certain Asian countries. Despite the lessening of anti-Jewish feeling in many places, the large communities of Eastern Europe were to suffer many changes in the seventeenth and eighteenth centuries. Their security was interrupted in 1648. In that year Bogdan Chmielnicki (1593–1657) was elected the leader of the Cossacks and he led a revolution against the Polish aristocracy. The Jews, some of whom were stewards of the great estates, were very much identified with the interests of the upper classes and took the brunt of the onslaught. It was a massacre. Probably as many as a quarter of the Jewish population of Poland was murdered during the course of the upheaval and many others were sold in the slave markets of Constantinople (today's Istanbul). Poland ceased to be a secure refuge.

History shows that instability promotes messianic yearnings, and this may explain the phenomenon of a second trauma which followed in the wake of the first. Shabbetai Zevi (1626–76), a gifted but unbalanced scholar, had attracted many followers. He had been born in Smyrna on the Ninth Day of *Av* (*Av* 9), the traditional birthdate of the Messiah. After the horrors of the Chmielnicki revolution, Jews everywhere were hoping for the immediate advent of a messianic redeemer. Shabbetai was expelled from his own community in 1651, but by 1665 he had been recognized as the Messiah by Nathan Benjamin Levi of Gaza (1644–80). Nathan of Gaza (in southern Palestine) believed that he himself was the Prophet Elijah, the forerunner. He sent messages throughout the Jewish world, promising that soon the Turkish Sultan would be deposed and that the Twelve Tribes of Israel would be united once more. The current difficulties he described as the "birth pangs of the Messiah ..." World Jewry was in an uproar. The date of redemption was set for June 18, 1666. A Christian contemporary described how he "perceived a strange transport in the Jews, none of them attending to any business... All their discourses, all their dreams and disposal of their affairs tended to no other design, but a reestablishment in the Land of Promise, to greatness and glory, wisdom and doctrine of the Messiah."[1] However, when Shabbetai landed near the Ottoman capital of Constantinople, he was promptly arrested. He was taken to the court of the Grand Vizier where he was given the choice between being put to death or converting to Islam. Shabbetai and his wife chose to become Muslims and he finally died in exile in Albania.

Amazingly, this was not the end of the matter. Nathan of Gaza continued to insist that Shabbetai was the Messiah and that his conversion was a part of the ongoing battle with the forces of evil. **Shabbetean** beliefs continued to be held in some quarters and some Jews followed their master into Islam, forming the *Dönmeh* ("Apostate sect"). A *Dönmeh* community existed in Istanbul until the mid twentieth century. Nonetheless, for most Jews, the whole episode was devastating. Shabbetai was not the Messiah. God had not sent his anointed one to save Israel and the world. It seemed as if *Talmudic* scholarship and traditional rabbinic learning had failed them. The Jews of Eastern Europe were looking for a new type of Judaism.

They found it in the teachings of Israel ben Eliezer (c.1700–60), known as the *Baal Shem Tov* ("Master of the Good Name") or Besht. He grew up in the Carpathian mountains (in present-day Romania) and his mystical preaching attracted a

Rabbis in Lodz, Poland, walking to the synagogue on Sabbath in 1915. The Sabbath is a day of rest and an occasion for prayer, study, and refreshment of the spirit. Synagogue services include readings from the Torah and the Books of the Prophets.

group of followers. He insisted that the study of *Torah* should be an act of devotion and that the whole of daily life could be an offering to God. In particular, he emphasized that worship should be a source of joy; he used to say that his disciples should serve God with gladness since a joyful man is overflowing with love for his fellows and for all God's creatures. The Besht's followers were known as the **Hasidim** ("pious ones") and the movement spread throughout Eastern Europe. Various new leaders emerged and, in the course of time, leadership became hereditary, handed down from father to son. By the beginning of the nineteenth century, probably almost half of Eastern Europe's Jewry identified itself with the new movement. *Hasidim* loved to explore the Kabbalah, the main Jewish mystic tradition. Once an esoteric tradition, with origins going back to the last days of the Tanakh, it had developed mainly in Sephardi lands. Scholars now believe that it both influenced and was in turn influenced by Islamic Sufism and Christian pietism. Kabbalah's prime books were *Sefer Bahir* (Book of Bahir) and the *Zohar* (Splendor). *Hasidim* tried to open up this hitherto secret world to ordinary Jews in the *Ashkenazi* sphere. But most of all, they derived from Kabbalah the values and attributes of devotion, adherence, wisdom, knowledge, and understanding.

Important characteristics of *Hasidism* included rejoicing and enthusiasm which became part of the religious experience of ordinary people. It was not long before distinct *Hasidic* sects arose, each one led by a **Tzaddik** ("Righteous Man"), who is believed to be the spiritual channel through which God's grace flows. By observing the *Tzaddik*, the *Hasid* can learn how God can be worshiped in every detail of life, from tying one's shoes to eating one's food or taking a nap. As the spiritual leader of his community, the *Tzaddik* holds mass audience, gives individual advice and is supported by the donations of the faithful. Tales circulated describing the miraculous saintliness of the *Tzaddikim* and collections of their homilies were published.

The Eastern European *Hasidic* groups were decimated by the Nazi Holocaust. Nonetheless the movement survived, particularly in the United States and in Israel. Adherents are perhaps the most visible segment of the strictly Orthodox community and the men in particular are readily identifiable by their dress (black hats, beards, side curls, black suits, ritual fringes, and magnificent fur hats on the Sabbath). Among the best known groups are the *Lubavich, Satmar, Belz, Bobover, Gur,* and *Vizhnitz* (each named after their town of origin).

However, not all Jews were persuaded by *Hasidism*. Many scholars disapproved of the *Hasidic* deviations from the traditional liturgy. They deplored the setting up of separate houses of worship away from the local synagogue and, most of all, they were appalled by the *Hasidic* neglect of painstaking textual study. These traditionalists were known as the *Mitnagdim* ("Opponents") and their leader was the learned *Gaon* of Vilna in Lithuania, Elijah ben Solomon Zalman (1720–97). The Vilna Gaon, as he was called, was himself a child prodigy and was regarded as a master of *Talmud* at the age of 13. He was determined to preserve traditional scholarship and he was a major figure in the revival of *Talmudic* study. There was bitter conflict between the *Mitnagdim* and the *Hasidim*. Books were burnt, decrees of excommunication were pronounced, and it was not unknown for parents to go through the rites of mourning if one of their sons joined an *Hasidic* sect.

The difference between the two groups is delightfully illustrated in a (possibly apocryphal) story about the Vilna Gaon. He was giving a tutorial and two boys were looking out of the window at a bird soaring through the sky. When asked what they were thinking, one boy replied that the bird made him think of the soul ascending towards Heaven. The reply was too reminiscent of *Hasidic* mysticism and the lad was told to leave the class. The other said that he was wondering what would happen if the bird dropped dead and fell on a fence boundary. To whom would the carcass belong? The Vilna Gaon was delighted: "God be praised for someone who knows what religion is about!" he said.

Today, hostility between the *Hasidim* and the *Mitnagdim* has largely disappeared. The *Hasidim* have also become learned *Talmudists* and, perhaps more importantly, a far greater threat to both these groups emerged with the advent of the Western **Enlightenment**. The Jews of Western Europe were being freed from their ancient civil disabilities and were being increasingly affected by secular culture. They were beginning to question such fundamental principles as the divine origin of *Torah*. This was an abomination to both *Mitnaged* and *Hasid*. Against it they were prepared to stand firm together and the late twentieth-century strictly Orthodox community contains both *Hasidic* and non-*Hasidic* members.

Enlightenment and Reform

While the *Mitnagdim* and the *Hasidim* were fighting their battles in Eastern Europe, great social changes were occurring in the West. In the Holy Roman Empire, under Emperor Joseph II (1741–90), an edict of toleration was issued. Jews were no longer to be confined to special places of residence, restricted to their own schools or made to wear distinctive clothing. Similarly, in 1791, the National Assembly of France granted full citizenship rights of the Jewish population and it was agreed that there should be full freedom of religion. Napoleon (1769–1821) went one step further, once he had taken over the French government. In 1806, he convened an Assembly of Jewish Notables and, the following year, he revived the Sanhedrin, the traditional supreme body of Jewish government. From then on the French Jewish community was organized much as if it were a department of the civil service.

Napoleon himself was defeated at the Battle of Waterloo in 1815, but, despite residual Christian anti-semitism, his reforms could not be undone. Several German and French intellectuals argued for the rights of the Jews and gradually additional freedoms were procured. In 1869 the North German parliament proclaimed Jewish emancipation and by 1871 all restrictions on occupation, franchise, marriage, or residence were removed. Meanwhile, in England, the Jews had been free to conduct their own religious life as they saw fit since the seventeenth century. Nonetheless, various religious tests existed which prevented Jews from taking a full part in the political and cultural life of the nation. These were all abolished during the course of the nineteenth century and in 1858 the first Jewish Member of Parliament took his seat in the House of Commons.

While these momentous social changes were taking place, the Jews themselves were experiencing an intellectual revolution. The most influential thinker of the Jewish Enlightenment was Moses Mendelssohn (1729–86). Encouraged by the Christian philosopher G. E. Lessing (1729–81), he taught that God's existence, His providence, and His gift of immortality could all be discovered by the use of natural reason. He believed that the mission of the Jews was to call attention to the Oneness of God and to be a constant reminder to the rest of humanity of the call of ethical monotheism.

He also called for freedom of worship and the removal of state interference in religious affairs. As he put it, "Do not hold out bribes or incentives to encourage people to adopt particular theologies. Allow everyone who does not disturb the peace ... to pray to God in his own way."[2] At the same time he encouraged the modernization of Jewish education; he translated the Pentateuch into German and wrote an extensive Biblical commentary. Through his leadership, German Jewry became acquainted with secular European culture. He himself remained a strictly observant Jew, yet his advocacy of Jewish emancipation brought another dilemma in its wake: how far could a Jew absorb the outside world's culture before he assimilated altogether? Was it just an accident, then, that four of Mendelssohn's own six children eventually converted to Christianity?

The Jewish Enlightenment completely changed the lives of Western Jewry. No longer were they restricted in residence (**ghetto**) or occupation. They became knowledgeable in the ways of the secular world and many came to feel that the traditional ways of worship were no longer suitable. One result, the Reform movement, started in Germany. The financier Israel Jacobson (1768–1828) built the first Reform Temple at Seesen. There the liturgy included prayers in German, as well as choral singing. Another similar congregation was started in Hamburg in 1818, which issued its own Prayer Book. This omitted all reference to the Messiah and to the restoration of the Twelve Tribes to the Holy Land. Members of the Temple saw themselves as loyal Germans and they owed no allegiance to any other place. Meanwhile, influenced by the historical thinking of the time, some religious leaders were denying the fundamental doctrine that the *Torah* was handed down in its entirety by God to Moses on Mount Sinai. They tried to study the history of Judaism with no religious preconceptions. Others were arguing that Judaism was simply a religious tradition of ethical monotheism and that many traditional practices no longer had any validity. They recommended modifications of the dietary laws, praying with the head uncovered, and even transferring the Sabbath from Saturday to Sunday to be more like their Christian fellow citizens.

The new movement spread rapidly. The first conference for Reform rabbis had taken place by 1838. The West London synagogue for Reform Jews was founded in 1841. A Reform Rabbinical Seminary was opened in Breslau in 1854, another in Hungary in 1867, and the *Berlin Hochschule* opened its doors in 1872.

However, increasingly, the United States was to be the main centre for Reform activities. The first American Reform Temple was founded in Charleston, South Carolina, in 1824. Its liturgy was similar to that of the Hamburg Temple and its founders described its purpose as to avoid anything that might disgust well educated Israelites. Later Reform Temples were built in most major American cities. A new American Reform Prayer Book was published and the first conference of American rabbis took place in Philadelphia in 1869. The Hebrew Union College, the first American Rabbinical Seminary, opened in 1875 in Cincinnati, Ohio. The principles of American Reform Judaism were laid down in Pittsburgh in 1885. It was agreed that the Jewish tradition should take account of the findings in modern scholarship, that only the moral laws of the Pentateuch were binding for all time, that Jews should no longer look for the coming of the Messiah or the restoration of the land of Israel, and that the dietary laws and the laws of ritual purity were anachronistic. This provided a credal framework for American Reform Judaism for the next fifty years. By the end of the nineteenth century, many Jews of North America were almost indistinguishable from their fellow citizens in dress, manners, education, and aspiration. In this century Reform Judaism has undergone further developments and a variety of credal platforms and new Prayer Books have been produced.

The Orthodox did not allow this transformation to take place without a fight. They were horrified by the new developments and feared that participation in secular culture could all too easily lead to assimilation. The best known German Orthodox thinker of the time was Samson Raphael Hirsch (1808–88). He himself had been educated at the University of Bonn. Nevertheless he defended Orthodoxy, arguing that the purpose of life was not to attain happiness, but to serve God. The *Torah*, he insisted, was of divine origin and must be the guiding principle of Jewish life. At the same time he believed that it was possible to be fully observant, while being conversant with modern culture. This position came to be known as Modern Orthodoxy. There could be no compromise on the doctrine of the God-given nature of the *Torah* and the Reform movement must be unequivocally condemned. At the same time, Jews could also have the benefit of a secular education and could enjoy the fruits of modern culture.

Although Modern Orthodoxy was highly influential in Western Europe, the Jews of Poland, Russia, and the Baltic States were less affected by it. Western Europe had longer traditions of democratic compromise; by contrast, in the more radical traditions of Eastern Europe, disaffected Jews chose socialist secularism as their preferred tool of protest against Orthodoxy. Change was inevitable, but it was to come not as a result of political emancipation, but in response to anti-semitism and the opportunity of an entirely new life across the Atlantic Ocean.

Anti-semitism and Zionism

It was hoped that anti-semitism would disappear with the transformation of Jewish life in Western Europe. This was not to be the case. Instead the nature of Jew-hatred altered. In the previous centuries, the Jews were regarded as social outcasts. The Christian Gospels taught that the Jews had rejected Jesus as the Messiah and had sent him to his crucifixion. The vast majority of Christians could not understand why the Jews persisted in their ancient faith since it had been superseded by Jesus' teaching. The Jews were seen as stubborn, obtuse, and blind to God's grace. Yet, if a Jew converted to Christianity, attitudes immediately changed. The Jew was no longer a Jew; he or she was a Christian. She/he gained all the rights and privileges of his/her new status and, provided she/he completely rejected his/her former beliefs, she/he became a fully accepted member of Christian society.

The very term "anti-semitism" was not used until the 1870s and it described a new prejudice. The inventor of the term, Wilhelm Marr (1818–1904), insisted that the Jews were not alien because of their religion, but because they were of a different and foreign race. He believed that modern history should be understood as an ongoing battle between "native Teutonic stock" and the Semitic foreigner. By 1881 it was being claimed that the Jewish physical type was a threat to the pure-bred German nation. Jews were described as innately mercenary, egoistic, materialistic, cowardly, and degenerate. These views were spread in such publications as *The Protocols of the Elders of Zion*. This was circulated in Russia from the late 1880s and was supposedly the documents of a Jewish organization bent on world domination. Although known to be a forgery, the *Protocols* are still circulated in Russia today and are enjoying new audiences in the Arab world and among some fanatic American groups.

In the late nineteenth century, anti-semitism became an important factor in European politics. It was used by beleaguered governments to focus discontent away from the authorities. In Russia, attacks on the Jews were described as **pogroms**. A pogrom was an onslaught on one sector of society by another and all too often it included rape and murder as well as the destruction of property. There was a series of pogroms against the Jewish community of Russia between 1881 and 1884 after the assassination of Czar Alexander II (1818–81). The civil powers did little to help the Jews—rather they encouraged the mob and many Jews felt that the only safety lay in emigration to the New World. A second wave of Russian pogroms occurred between 1903 and 1906 and there was a third outbreak during the Russian Revolution and the subsequent civil war. Altogether it has been estimated that between 1917 and 1921, as many as 150,000 Jewish people were killed by units of both the Red and the White Armies. It was not surprising that the Jews of Eastern Europe were anxious to leave. Between 1881 and the outbreak of World War I in 1914, approximately two million settled in the United States, a further 350,000 in Western Europe, 200,000 in the United Kingdom, 40,000 in South Africa, 115,000 in the Argentine, and 100,000 in Canada.

Western Europe was also not immune to Jew-hatred. The Dreyfus case brought it to international notice. Alfred Dreyfus (1859–1935) was a high ranking French Jewish army officer, who was accused of high treason and sentenced to life imprisonment. He consistently protested that he was innocent and it was eventually discovered that his conviction was based on false documents. Nevertheless, when he was tried again in 1899 a second guilty verdict was returned and he was only finally vindicated in 1906. The episode divided French public opinion; many found it impossible to believe that a Jew could also be a loyal Frenchman. A young journalist, Theodor Herzl (1860–1904), described the scene of the conviction vividly: "The wild screams of the street mob near the building of the military school where it was ordered that Dreyfus be deprived of his rank, still resound in my ears... "[3]

Herzl became convinced that the only solution to anti-semitism was the foundation of a Jewish State. Palestine was chosen as the site for this Jewish state because this is where Jewry last ruled itself, and because of the biblical connections. The old dream of returning to the Promised Land had been retained in the Jewish community and was enshrined in the liturgy. It was still believed that in the days of the Messiah, the Twelve Tribes would be gathered together again and the Temple would be rebuilt in Jerusalem. As early as 1882, after the first Russian pogroms, a group of Jews had left for Palestine to establish themselves as shopkeepers, artisans, and farmers. Herzl himself argued for the creation of a Jewish State by international agreement. He convened the First Zionist Conference in Basle in 1897 and devoted the rest of his short life to drumming up diplomatic support. In fact, he himself was willing to consider other locations besides Palestine. The British were prepared to offer a tract of Uganda in Africa to the Jews and, after a visit to the poverty-stricken Jewish villages of Russia, Herzl was so desperate that he was prepared to accept. However, the proposal aroused a storm of protest at the Sixth Zionist Conference and, just before his death, Herzl was forced to affirm his commitment to Palestine.

The small Jewish population in Palestine mainly consisted of religious pilgrims in the Holy Cities, and was vastly outnumbered by Palestine's predominantly Muslim Arab population. Furthermore, the land was under Ottoman Turkish rule. Some Zionists, like the British Jewish author Israel Zangwill, seeing the indigenous Arabs as mainly itinerant nomads, called Palestine "A land without people for a people without a land." Others, though, were more far-sighted: in 1891 Ahad Ha-Am warned that Jews would not realize their dreams unless they respected the rights and aspirations of Palestinian Arabs. So with the benefit of hindsight it seems a clash was inevitable.

There is an old saying that where there are four Jews there are six opinions. This was certainly true in the Zionist movement. The **World Zionist Organization**, founded by Herzl, was the umbrella body. Socialist Jews also became members of the *Poale Zion* (the Labour Zionist party). Those of the Orthodox who were willing to participate joined the *Mizrakhi* party, which was dedicated to the preservation of strictly Orthodox ways within the new State. However, the majority of Western and Eastern (except for the Orthodox) delegates to the Zionist conferences were entirely secular in outlook and this caused considerable conflict with the Orthodox Jewish establishment in Europe. Prominent early Zionists included Aaron David Gordon (1856–1922) who was determined to encourage agricultural as well as commercial settlement, the writers Ahad Ha-Am (1856–1927) and Chaim Nachman Bialik (1873–1934) who were intent on producing a Hebrew rather than a Yiddish culture, and the socialists Nahman Syrkin (1868–1924) and Ber Borochov (1881–1917) who were encouraging the creation of collective agricultural settlements *(Kibbutzim)* and the growth of trade unionism. In the early days of Zionism, many of the strictly Orthodox were uneasy. In 1912 they organized the *Agudat Israel* to unite rabbis and lay people against the new movement. They maintained that the Ingathering of the Exiles could not take place until the Messiah had appeared and that it was forbidden to anticipate or to force divine deliverance. Even after the Holocaust, there were those who argued that the Zionist commitment to the ingathering of the displaced Jews of Europe was misguided since it is not possible to determine God's plan for his Chosen People prior to the coming of the Messiah.

After World War I, the newly formed League of Nations agreed that Britain should administer Palestine. The Jewish population continued to grow. In 1917, in the Balfour Declaration, the British government had promised its support for a Jewish State in Palestine. By the late 1920s, the various socialist groups had joined together to form the Israel Labour Movement. Chaim Weizman (1874–1952) was President of the World Zionist Organization and he tried to cooperate with the British. Meanwhile the Arab inhabitants of the land had become increasingly nervous of Jewish immigration and by 1936 they were launching offensives against the settlers. The situation was becoming impossible. In 1937, a British Royal Commission suggested that Palestine be partitioned between the two groups, but this was rejected in the White Paper of 1939 and Jewish immigration was substantially cut back. Nothing further could be done while the battles of World War II waged. And meanwhile calamity befell the Jews of Europe.

Judaism in the Twentieth Century

In the 1930s both Europe and the United States were in the throes of serious economic depression. The situation was particularly bad in Germany where between 1930 and 1933 more than six million people were unemployed. The government was

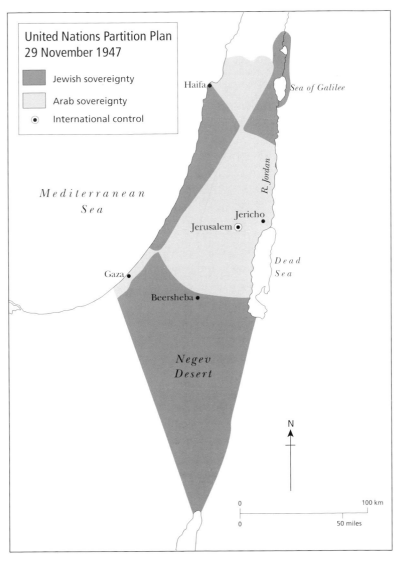

United Nations Partition Plan
29 November 1947

Jewish sovereignty

Arab sovereignty

⊙ International control

Haifa

Sea of Galilee

Mediterranean Sea

R. Jordan

Jericho

Jerusalem ⊙

Dead Sea

Gaza

Beersheba

Negev Desert

N

0   100 km

0   50 miles

The State of Israel was proclaimed in 1948 after British withdrawal. In the face of Arab opposition, the UN had drawn up a plan whereby Palestine was to be divided into a Jewish state, an Arab state, and a small internationally administered zone around Jerusalem (see p. 72).

unstable and in 1933, after several ineffective coalitions, Adolf Hitler (1885–1945) was appointed Chancellor. Hitler was the leader of the National Socialist Party, the Nazis; his ideology was based on a fusion of anti-Communism and anti-semitism. He was convinced that all Jews were degenerates and parasites and he argued in his book, *Mein Kampf* ("My Struggle"), that it was the treachery of the Jews which caused Germany to lose World War I. He perceived the Jews as a demonic people, who were seeking world wide domination. As he himself put it:

> The black-haired Jewish youth lies in wait for hours on end, satanically glaring at and spying on the unsuspicious girl whom he plans to seduce, adulterating her blood and removing her from the bosom of her own people ... the Jews were responsible for bringing Negros into the Rhineland, with the ultimate intention of bastardising the white race which they hate and thus lowering its cultural and political level so that the Jew might dominate ...[4]

Once the Nazis had gained power, a series of anti-Jewish regulations came into force. Jews were deprived of citizenship, were forbidden to marry, or have sexual relations with, German citizens, and were compelled to register their property. Then, on the night of November 9, 1938, the government organized a concerted attack on all Jewish businesses and communal institutions. Synagogues were burnt to the ground, shops were destroyed and many individual Jews were murdered. The events of *Kristallnacht* (the Night of Broken Glass) made it clear to the Jews of Germany that they could expect no mercy from the Nazis. They tried to find means of escaping from the country with their families, but it was not easy. The United States also had many unemployed and was accepting very few new immigrants. The British had curtailed Jewish settlement in Palestine and the countries of Western Europe were not inclined to take in any more refugees. Families resorted to desperate measures, sending their children abroad without them to distant relations or on *Kindertransports* (child-transports).

All too many, however, were forced to stay and once World War II had broken out in September 1939, there was no escape. The German armies overran Europe and everywhere they continued their persecution of the Jews. In Poland there was a large Jewish population and everywhere the Jews were seized and were forced to participate in a massive work program. These slave laborers toiled for seven days a week, were dressed in little more than rags, and were given totally inadequate rations. Then, once the Nazis had invaded Russia in 1941, special squadrons known as *Einsatzgruppen* were coopted to deal with the Jews. In each conquered town, the Jews were rounded up, marched out to the countryside and shot. It has been estimated that between October 1941 and December 1942 1.2 million people were murdered in this way.

However, this was not sufficiently systematic or efficient for the Nazi leaders. At the Wannsee Conference on January 20, 1942 the "final solution of the Jewish question" was outlined and explained. A network of concentration and extermination camps was set up. From all over Europe, the Jews were rounded up and deported "for resettlement" in the East. Initially they were crammed into ghetto areas in the major cities. From there they were transferred to concentration camps. There, in the camps of Chelmno, Auschwitz, Sobibor, Majdanek, Treblinka, and Belzec, the young and fit were selected for work while the elderly, the infirm, and children were sent to the gas chambers. The workers lived in miserable conditions, in a state of perpetual fear, cold, and hunger. Once they themselves became too weak to labor they too were sent to their deaths. The camp at Auschwitz, in southern Poland, could hold 140,000 prisoners and it had five crematoria which could dispose of 10,000 bodies a day. The whole operation was conducted with ruthless efficiency and even when Germany was clearly losing the war, nothing was allowed to hinder the transportation of Jewish civilians to the camps. Altogether, it is generally thought that six million Jews died in this Holocaust.

In many places the Jews did their best to resist. There were several small-scale rebellions in the concentration camps and the inmates of the Warsaw ghetto held out for several weeks against the might of the German *Reich*. Nonetheless, in most places the Jews were poor and isolated; they were surrounded by hostile neighbors and they were abandoned by the rest of the world. They had no chance. By the end of World War II, European Jewry had effectively been decimated. The old synagogues, *Yeshivot*, and centers of Jewish learning were destroyed for ever.

The demise of Eastern European Jewry and the creation of the State of Israel are two interrelated events. World Jewry rallied to the Zionist cause. Jews had fought in the British, United States, and Canadian armies but the problem of the refugee concentration camp survivors seemed to be insoluble. Also, the situation in Palestine itself was impossible. A sizeable sector of the Jewish population, under the leadership of Menahem Begin (1913–92), were prepared to employ terrorist tactics against the British administrators. On November 6, 1944, Lord Moyne, the British minister for Middle Eastern affairs, was assassinated. A rift developed between the leader of the World Zionist Organization, Chaim Weizman, and Begin over the bombing of the King David Hotel in Jerusalem, but the campaign of violence continued and culminated in the hanging of two British army sergeants. The British could stand it no more. They handed over the responsibility to the newly formed United Nations.

The Americans backed the Zionists. The President, Harry S. Truman, was both personally sympathetic and anxious to secure the Jewish vote in the 1948 Presidential election. The question was first discussed in May 1947 and on November 29, the United Nations General Assembly, with both Russian and American support, agreed that Palestine should be partitioned into a Jewish and an Arab state and that Jerusalem should be an international zone (see map, p. 69). Zionists accepted the principle of partition, but Arabs did not, reasoning that partition would deny them their "national rights" over the whole land, as they claimed was guaranteed by the United Nations charter.

Immediately the Arabs began to attack the Jewish settlements, but, under the leadership of David ben Gurion (1886–

The Western Wall is the surviving part of the outer wall of the Temple in Jerusalem. Regular services have been held there since the Middle Ages, and today it remains a place of prayer for all Jews.

1973), the Jews consolidated their position. On May 14, 1948, the independence of the Jewish State of Palestine was declared, based both on the resolution of the United Nations and on "national and intrinsic right." The new nation was to be called Israel. Still the conflict continued and by 1949 the Israelis held large tracts of land beyond the frontiers designated by the United Nations. An armistice was eventually signed between Israel on the one side and Jordan, Syria, Egypt, and Lebanon on the other. The peace was to be permanent.

War broke out again in 1956, in 1967 (when the Israelis captured Jerusalem and the West Bank of the Jordan, the Gaza

Strip, and the Golan Heights), and in 1973. Even today the problem of Palestinian refugees, who constituted most of the pre-war Arab population of Palestine, has still not been solved. In the 1947–8 war, more than half a million Arab refugees fled from their homes. Some found sanctuary in the surrounding countries, but too many live in temporary camps which are a constant source of discontent and guerrilla activity.

Nonetheless, today the State of Israel is perhaps more secure than at any time in its existence. Since 1978 the Egyptians have participated in the peace process. Then in 1982, Israeli forces invaded Lebanon in order to destroy Arab guerrilla bases. This destabilized the area. Five years later, Palestinians in the occupied territories began a concentrated program of resistance (intifada) which involved stone throwing, ambushes, and selective strikes. The Israelis realized that compromises would have to be made. Beginning in 1991 further peace talks have taken place between the government and the Palestinian Liberation Organization which have raised hopes that an autonomous Arab Palestine could be created which would coexist peaceably with Israel. Talks were interrupted and the whole of Israeli society was rocked by the assassination of Prime Minister Rabin by an extremist Jewish student in 1995. Peace developments may also have been threatened by the victory of the hardline Likud party in the 1996 Israeli elections. Nonetheless, despite enormous problems, there is no doubt that the international community recognizes the existence of the Jewish State of Israel and, at the same time, with pious Jews everywhere "prays for the peace of Jerusalem."[5]

<table>
<tr><td>

Jewish Beliefs and Practices

</td><td>

4

</td></tr>
</table>

God and *Torah*

Before embarking on a discussion of the Jewish religion, it is essential to emphasize again that by no means all people who identify as Jews are religious. There is also a wide variety of religious practice and belief within the community. What follows here is a brief description of traditional Orthodox Judaism since that is the form of Judaism which has been followed for hundreds of years. At the same time it must be remembered that many Jews in America, the home of the largest community in the world, are not Orthodox, and the Reform and Conservative movements follow their own customs and  liturgies. Yet these, too, are ultimately rooted in the Hebrew Bible. In addition, many Jews practice no religion at all.

The essential belief of Judaism is that God is One. The primary prayer of the Jewish faith is the assertion of this conviction. It is known as the **Shema** from the Hebrew word for "Hear!" When they rise in the morning, when they go to bed at night, and, hopefully, on their deathbed, most Jews recite, "*Shema Israel, Adonai Eloheynu, Adonai Ehad!*" (Hear O Israel, the Lord our God, the Lord is One). This is the supreme truth. It is the essential message of the Scriptures and it was this unique insight that God gave to the Jewish people. As it is written in the Book of Deuteronomy, "To you it was shown that the Lord is God, there is no one other besides Him."[1]

The One God is the source of the universe. The Book of Genesis, the first book of the Bible, begins with the sentence, "In the beginning, God created the heavens and the earth."[2] It goes on to describe how He labored for six days making night and day, the world and the sky, the seas and the dry land, vegetation for food, the sun, the moon and the stars and all the creatures. Finally He created human beings in His own image. Scholars and laymen have argued for centuries about what it means, but most agree that in the Jewish world view, humans, like their Creator, are endowed with free will. They can choose between good and evil. Some even describe history as an ongoing partnership between God and man. And because we reflect God's image, human life is considered sacrosanct in Judaism. On the seventh day He rested and this became known as the Sabbath (see page 15).

The creation is not regarded merely as an historical event. Creation is seen as an ongoing process. Every seed that germinates, every change in the weather and every new birth is evidence of God's involvement with the universe. At the same time He transcends His creation. As the Book of Isaiah has it, "My thoughts are not your thoughts, neither are your ways My ways, says the Lord. For as the heavens are higher than the earth, so are My ways higher than your ways and My thoughts higher than your thoughts."[3]

According to the Genesis account of the creation, once God had done His work, He saw that it was good. It was a reflection of His own nature. As the Psalmist wrote, "The Lord is gracious and merciful, slow to anger and abounding in steadfast love."[4] This raises the question of how evil came into the world. Throughout Jewish history, there has been intense speculation about this and various alternatives have been raised. The problem has become particularly acute since the horrors of the Holocaust have been revealed. As the source of everything, God is regarded in the tradition as being all-powerful and all-knowing, as well as all-good. It is hard to understand why, if God knew about the Nazi Final Solution and if He was able to stop it, He did not choose to do so. This does not seem compatible with

His infinite compassion. Again attempts have been made to
resolve this dilemma. For most, however, it is an insoluble problem. God's ways are inscrutable. In the Bible, when Job was
struck down with a series of undeserved misfortunes, he
demanded an explanation. God's response was, "Where were you
when I laid the foundations of the earth?"[5] For the pious, this is
the only possible answer. The existence of evil remains the ultimate theological mystery.

The Jews believe that they are the Chosen People of the One
God. This does not mean that God shows favoritism. The tradition stresses that chosenness involves responsibility as well as
privilege. The relationship of God with the Jews is characterized
as a covenantal two-sided bargain. The deal is spelt out in the
Book of Exodus: "If you will obey My voice and keep My
covenant, you shall be my own possession among all the peoples."[6] In order to preserve the relationship, the Jews must keep
God's law. The clear connection between obedience to the law
and chosenness is emphasized in the liturgy. In the synagogue,
when each reader is called up to the scroll of the *Torah* (here the
Five Books of Moses), he recites, "Blessed art Thou, O Lord our
God, King of the Universe, who hast chosen us from all peoples
and hast given us Thy law."[7]

Torah is the Hebrew word for "law." In Judaism it is used to
refer to the Pentateuch, but in its broader sense it can also
include the whole body of Written and Oral Law, or the entire
Jewish way of life. *Torah* covers every detail—foods that are permitted, proper clothing, conduct towards fellow Jews, dealings
with all human beings, the role of women, the duties of parents
and children, the festivals which must be celebrated, and the
fasts that must be observed.

Nonetheless, the sages made an important distinction
between the revelation of the Pentateuch and that of the rest of
Scripture. The Pentateuch is thought to have been given directly by God to Moses and it is thus held in the most reverence. It
is written by hand on a long scroll, rolled and kept in the *ark*,
the central focal point of the synagogue. When it is removed
from the ark, the congregation stands and it is treated with

ART FOCUS

Synagogue Design

JEWS HAVE TENDED TO BUILD their synagogues in the style of their host nations. Thus the synagogues of Europe, built in the Middle Ages, were often constructed in the Romanesque or Gothic style. In Poland in the seventeenth and eighteenth centuries, village synagogues were often simple wooden buildings with tiled roofs. In the nineteenth century, in affluent Jewish communities, grandiose edifices in the Moorish, Egyptian, Gothic, or Classical style became usual. In recent years, particularly in the United States, the trend has been for modern, exciting buildings—a famous example being the synagogue designed by Frank Lloyd Wright for the Beth Shalom congregation of Elkins Park, Pennsylvania.

In Hebrew the synagogue is called the *Bet Ha-Knesset*, or assembly house, which speaks more of its historic social function than its spiritual significance. The Yiddish-speaking communities of Eastern Europe used to describe the building as a 'shul'— literally a school. A synagogue is, therefore, a place of study and learning as well as a place of prayer. In contrast, the Temple in Jerusalem was believed to be the House of God. In a very real sense God was believed to dwell in the Holy of Holies, the Temple's innermost sanctum, and sacrifices were offered in the Temple courts three times a day. Since the destruction of the Temple in 70 C.E., Jews have not practiced sacrifice. Instead worship is offered to God through regular prayer and occasional fasting.

The organization of the synagogue building reflects its use. The focus of the structure is the ark, a large cupboard sometimes richly decorated, which contains the Scrolls of the Law. The ark is the nearest point of the building to Jerusalem, the holy city. The Scrolls of the Law are written by hand and contain the text of the Pentateuch, the first five books of the Hebrew Scriptures.

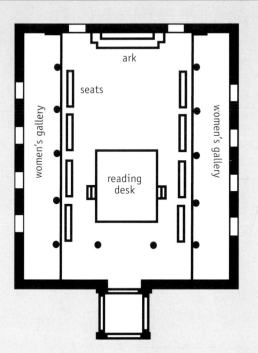

In the traditional synagogue, much of the central space is taken up by the reading desk, and the seating is mainly along the sides facing inward. The columns support the women's gallery.

They are read at the morning service in such a way that the whole text is heard every year. In the center of the building is the *bimah*, the dais, from which the service is conducted. Any Jewish man (and among the non-Orthodox any woman as well) may conduct all, or part of, the liturgical service and members of the congregation are formally called up to read from the Scrolls. In Orthodox and Modern Orthodox synagogues, provision is made for the women to sit apart from the men, in order that they can pray without distraction or disturbing the men from their prayers.

utmost reverence. The text is divided into 54 portions and every week one section is read aloud. Its importance in Jewish life cannot be overestimated. In the words of the liturgy, "It is the tree of life to those who grasp it and those who hold it are truly happy… "[8]

Altogether there are 613 commandments in the Pentateuch and these have been explained and interpreted in the vast treasury of Oral Law. Still later this great body of law was codified. The strictly Orthodox regard the whole *Torah*, Written, Oral, and Codes, to be the word of God. It is what separates the Jews from the other nations. As we have seen, the non-Orthodox (the Conservative and the Reform) take a more liberal view. Nonetheless, it is obedience to God's law which has defined the identity of the Jews and ensured their survival, while so many other religious groups of the ancient world have disappeared. The rabbis indulged in theological speculation, but it was not regarded as important. What counted was faithfulness to God's covenant. The point is movingly illustrated in a well known story about the Holocaust. One evening, amidst all the squalor of the camp, a group of scholars gathered together to put God on trial. How could He tolerate what was happening to His people? The debate raged all night and, in the end, there could be only one conclusion. God had somehow failed His chosen. The Jewish religion was based on a falsehood. As the discussion drew to a close, dawn was breaking and another day of cruel work lay ahead. All the participants stood and prayed the traditional morning service together.

From Day to Day

Services are held three times a day in Orthodox synagogues. This corresponds with the time the sacrifices were offered in the Temple in Jerusalem. For the service to take place, there must be at least ten adult men present. Women traditionally do not count towards this quorum and, today, it is often difficult to raise the necessary number. Non-Orthodox Jews, who insist on absolute equality between the sexes, do count women in. Most Reform Temples (as they are called), however, do not hold daily services.

At the core of the liturgy are the two prayers, the *Shema* ("Hear O Israel...") and the *Amidah*, originally a series of 18 blessings. The *Shema* declares the essential unity of God and the necessity of remembering His commandments. They are to be "bound as frontlets between your eyes and you shall write them on the doorposts of your house."[9] Jews fulfill this by putting on **phylacteries** (tefillin) and by nailing a **mezuzah** to their doorposts. In Orthodox Judaism only men wear phylacteries, but in Reform Judaism women, especially women rabbis, sometimes also wear them. Phylacteries are special boxes containing certain Biblical verses written by hand on parchment, which are attached to straps. One box is placed over the head so it sits squarely between the eyes and the other is wound around the left arm so that it lies against the heart. These phylacteries are put on during the morning service every day, except for the Sabbath and on festivals. The *mezuzah* is another small box containing parchment. On the parchment is written the first two paragraphs of the *Shema* prayer. The box is nailed on the right-hand doorpost. Almost all Jews who have any connection with Judaism have a *mezuzah* by their front door, while the strictly Orthodox have one on every door in the house (except the bathroom door). Both the phylacteries and the *mezuzah* are visible signs which remind the pious of their duty toward God and recall their awesome obligations as members of the chosen people.

The blessings of the *Amidah* prayer are traditionally recited while standing. They include a request for the restoration of the Temple; God is thanked for His many mercies and peace is asked for the people of Israel. In Reform Judaism the prayer for peace is asked for Israel and the whole world. Other important prayers in the daily service include the ***Kaddish*** and the *Alenu*. The *Kaddish* is an expression of longing for the establishment of God's sovereignty over the earth. It is said at the end of each major section of the liturgy and by mourners at the end of the service. Since it is a religious obligation to recite *Kaddish* for 11 months after the death of a close relative and since it can only be said in the religious quorum, this does something to guarantee the presence of ten worshipers at the daily service. The *Alenu* prayer proclaims the Kingship of God over all the world and it concludes the service.

Although the synagogue is the central communal institution of the Jewish faith, the home remains the real focus of religious life. Traditionally women are exempted from the positive timebound commandments (such as attending the daily services) because their role as homemaker and mother is so crucial. Among the Orthodox, every detail of daily life is covered by the commandments. This even includes food and clothing. One of the most recognizable signs of a male Jew is the skull cap, the *yarmulke* or *kippah*. The strictly Orthodox have it on at all times, but the Progressive tend only to wear it for prayer. Interestingly, the custom is not ancient. It only goes back to about the twelfth century C.E. and it was probably only introduced to distinguish Jewish from Christian practice (since Christian men always pray with their heads uncovered). Orthodox men also generally have beards. This is because the Book of Leviticus forbids the cutting of the corner of the facial hair.[10] It is also customary to allow the side locks to grow.

Another element of Orthodox appearance is the wearing of fringes. According to the *Torah*, the Israelites were instructed to "make tassels on the corner of their garments... it shall be to you a tassel to look upon and to remember all the commandments."[11] This is fulfilled by wearing an undergarment (*talit*) with fringes (*tzitzit*) on the four corners. For Modern Orthodox and Reform Jews the *talit* is a prayer-shawl, an overgarment. It is worn by women as well as men in Reform Judaism. The fringes of the *talit* are tied in a particular way to symbolize the numerical value of the Name of God. Since it is an undergarment, it is not normally seen although often a fringe is brought out above the trouser waistband and tucked into a pocket. Similar fringes are put on the four corners of the shawl which is worn for prayer in the synagogue. Orthodox women's dress is characterized by modesty. Married women are expected to keep their heads covered at all times and, particularly among the *Hasidim*, this is fulfilled by wearing a wig. In addition, men may not wear women's clothes nor women men's; this means that young Orthodox women are not to be seen wearing garments such as jeans.

If there is a single factor which has kept the Jewish people separate from the other nations, it is their food laws. Muslims inherited the idea of ritually pure food from the Jews, but most Christians by contrast regarded the strictures as null and void, as they believed the New Covenant superseded the Old. Not only are certain categories of food completely forbidden, even permitted animals and birds must be slaughtered in a particular way and milk foods must not be eaten with meat foods. This means, in effect, that all secular restaurant food and everything prepared in Gentile houses is non-*kosher* (ritually unfit to eat). According to the creation story in the Book of Genesis, the first human beings were vegetarians. Meat eating was only permitted after the Great Flood.[12] However, even then it was hedged round with so many restrictions that many authorities teach that in the days of the Messiah, humanity will return to vegetarianism. Only animals which have both a cloven hoof and chew the cud may be eaten and only birds which are commonly used for food qualify. Pigs, for example, are forbidden because they do not chew the cud and all birds of prey are non-*kosher*. The creature must be slaughtered by a qualified butcher. It is killed by a quick downward slice to the throat and hung so that the blood is immediately drained off. This is because eating the blood is not allowed. There are no specific rules of slaughter for fish, but not all sea creatures are permitted—only those with both fins and scales. Thus observant Jews do not eat any form of shellfish or eel.

In three places in the Pentateuch is written the commandment, "You shall not seethe the kid in its mother's milk."[13] This has been interpreted to mean that meat and dairy food may not be eaten together. Since minute particles of food can permeate crockery and cutlery, the observant housewife has two completely different sets of plates and saucepans. There must even be separate washing up bowls, draining boards, and preparation areas. Today, in strictly observant homes, it is not uncommon to see two sinks, two refrigerators and even two dishwashers. It also means that no manufactured foods can enter the house unless they are guaranteed to be *kosher*—that the rules of slaughter have been observed and that there is no intermingling of milk and meat. Many mass produced products today carry a certificate which shows that every stage of the processing has been inspected by a recognized religious authority.

It is often argued that the *kosher* food laws were developed for reasons of health. Pork is said to be forbidden, for example, because it can be a host for tapeworm. In fact no such explanation is given in the *Torah*. The laws of *Kashrut*, together with the laws for clothing and for every other aspect of daily life, are believed to have been laid down by God for His Chosen People. That, for the Orthodox, is the end of the matter. Among the observant, Jewish living in every detail is a reminder of the special relationship which exists between God and Israel. It calls for no other justification. However, it must be remembered that this level of observance is only practiced by a small number within the community.

The food laws are a particularly interesting illustration of the wide variety which exists within the community. For the very Orthodox, food is only *kosher* if it is approved by one of their own rabbinical authorities. Most Modern Orthodox, however, would accept any *kosher* authority and some may make various compromises in their own lives. So, for example, they might keep a *kosher* home, but eat any vegetarian food out. Or they might eat anything out. The laws of *Kashrut* are also increasingly being practiced by the Conservatives and the Reform. Some keep *kosher* homes; some merely avoid pork and shellfish. Vegetarianism, both for religious and for health reasons, is on the increase. Many other Jews simply ignore the food laws, reasoning that they have no moral validity, other than reminding people they are Jewish. Thus there is a full spectrum of observance.

From Year to Year

Traditionally Jewish life is dominated by the regular rhythm of the weekly Sabbath and the annual fast days and festivals. Because the Jewish calendar year is based on a lunar calendar, while the secular year is solar, these yearly celebrations do not seem to occur on the same day every year. The 12 Jewish months contain only 354 days and the shortfall is made up by adding a thirteenth month every few years. This ensures that the festivals occur at roughly the same time of year although not on the same secular date.

An Orthodox Sabbath has already been described in the first chapter. It occurs on Saturday, the seventh day of the week, because God himself rested from the work of creation on the seventh day.[14] It starts on Friday evening and ends after the stars appear on Saturday. For the full 25 hours it is a time of rest, a day of pleasure and delight. It begins with the mother of the household lighting the Sabbath candles and it ends the following evening with *Havdalah*, a ceremony involving wine, spices, a blessing, and a special lighted candle. The spices refresh the soul; the lighting of the candle symbolizes the end of the Sabbath; and the blessing thanks God for the distinction He has made between the sacred and the secular. The Sabbath is a time to enjoy friends and family, to study the *Torah*, and for husbands and wives to make love to one another, and to worship God. For many Jews today the traditional restrictions seem confining and oldfashioned. Nonetheless, the Sabbath is still kept to a greater or lesser extent among all the denominations. Sharing Sabbath meals, attending synagogue, and taking a walk together as a family provides a regular, tranquil interlude in their busy lives.

According to the Book of Deuteronomy, the Jewish people are to celebrate three **pilgrim festivals** every year: "Three times a year all your males shall appear before the Lord your God at a place which He will choose: at the festival of unleavened bread (Passover), at the feast of **Weeks** (*Shavuot*), and at the feast of booths (*Sukkot*)."[15] When the Temple was still standing, thousands of Jews went up to Jerusalem to offer sacrifices on these days. All three feasts have agricultural connotations as well as commemorating events in Jewish history. Passover, the spring festival, celebrates the start of the barley harvest as well as the liberation of the Jews from slavery in Egypt. It lasts for seven days (eight outside the land of Israel) and during this time, observant Jews eat nothing made with raising agents. This means that the whole house must be cleaned from top to bottom and special Passover cutlery and crockery must be brought out. On the first night, a special Passover meal (*seder*) is eaten during which the story of God's rescue of the Jews is told once more. Even the most secular attend a Passover meal and often have the most vivid childhood memories of the occasion. It is an opportunity for the whole extended family to get together and the evening ends with the long-cherished hope, "Next year in Jerusalem!"[16] Unlike most festivals, which center on the synagogue, the highpoint of Passover (*Pesach*), the *seder* meal, takes place at home. It is suffused with vividly contrasting symbols. Salt water (for tears) and horseradish (for bitterness) hark back to the days when Jews were slaves in Egypt. Yet the mandatory four cups of wine and copious cushions remind them that they are now free. As for eggs and fresh greens, these symbolize the hope of spring, rebirth, and fertility. It is said that the Christian Easter is based on the Jewish Passover, and certainly both festivals tend to fall at around the same time each year.

Shavuot celebrates the end of the barley harvest and occurs seven weeks after Passover. It also commemorates the giving of the *Torah* to Moses on Mount Sinai so, in a real sense, it is the birthday of the Jewish religion. It is the custom to eat milk foods on *Shavuot* because, like milk, the *Torah* nourishes everyone from the very young to the very old, and traditionally it is the time when boys and girls graduate from the synagogue religious school, having completed their formal religious education. Among the Reform, the ceremony of confirmation has been introduced for sixteen-year-olds as an incentive to stay in school beyond the **Bar/Bat Mitzvah** age (see next section). *Sukkot*, the feast of tabernacles, takes place in the autumn. It is a harvest festival as well as a reminder of the Jews' wanderings in the wilderness before they reached the Promised Land. They are supposed to live in a tabernacle (a temporary booth or hut) for the full eight (or nine outside Israel) days of the festival and there are detailed specifications as to how the structure should be built. At any rate, main meals should be eaten there, but in colder climates there is no obligation to sleep in it. Jews are also instructed how to make a *lulav*, a bundle of palm, willow and myrtle branches. Holding this in one hand and a citron (or *etrog*, a lemon-like fruit) in the other, they wave the *lulav* in all directions in the synagogue to symbolize God's control of all space. On the final day, the annual cycle of *Torah* reading is ended and a new cycle is begun. This is a cause of enormous rejoicing. The *Torah* scrolls are carried in procession around the synagogue amidst laughter and joy. In *Hasidic* communities, so great is the enthusiasm that it is not unusual for the procession to spill out onto the street.

There are also various minor and joyous festivals, particularly popular with children, the two best known being *Hanukkah*, the feast of lights, and **Purim**, the feast of Esther. In recent years *Hanukkah* has assumed considerable prominence because it occurs at much the same time as the Christian and commercial festival of Christmas. It celebrates the victory of Judas Maccabeus over the Hellenizing Seleucid kings of the second century B.C.E. It lasts for eight nights; presents are exchanged and an additional candle is lit every night. *Purim* occurs in the late winter and commemorates the escape of the Jewish people from the murderous designs of the wicked Haman who, according to the Biblical Book of Esther, wanted to destroy the Persian Jewish community. It is celebrated in the synagogue with readings and pageants.

The most important solemn days begin with the **New Year** (**Rosh Hashanah**) in the fall. This is the start of the Ten Days of Penitence which conclude with the Day of Atonement (*Yom Kippur*). The *Mishnah* teaches that all human beings pass before God on the New Year and are subject to judgment. A very small proportion are seen to be fully righteous and another group is immediately rejected as irredeemably wicked. The vast majority

*One of the three Pilgrim festivals, Sukkot commemorates God's
protection of the Israelites as they traveled through the wilderness
toward the promised land of Canaan. These schoolchildren hold in one
hand the* lulav *(a bundle made up of a palm branch, myrtle twigs, and
willow twigs) and the* etrog *(a citrus fruit) in the other. The plants are
waved toward the four compass points, the earth and sky, while God is
praised and acknowledged as the unmoving center of creation.*

are in the middle. They have ten days to repent of their evil ways
and to purge themselves in the great fast of Yom Kippur. On
Rosh Hashanah, the **shofar** (ram's horn) is blown. This makes a
strange, unearthly sound which calls the people to repentence.

As the great twelfth-century philosopher, Maimonides, put it, the *shofar* is commanding "Awake you sinners and ponder your deeds; remember your Creator, forsake evil and return to God."[17] The Day of Atonement is the most solemn day in the Jewish year. Every adult Jew, male and female, is expected to fast from sunset until nightfall the next day and, by this means, atonement for sin is made. The observant spend the whole day in synagogue praying for forgiveness. Even the more secular frequently attend the services on *Rosh Hashanah* and *Yom Kippur*. Jews who never go at any other time remain fascinated by the ritual and symbolism and the synagogues are full.

Other fasts include the Ninth Day of *Av* (*Tisha B'Av*), which commemorates the destruction of the Temple by the Babylonians in 586 B.C.E. and by the Romans in 70 C.E. This is not generally observed by the Reform, on the grounds that they neither expect nor desire the rebuilding of the Temple, although in recent years it has been revived. Less important are the fast of *Tammuz* which commemorates the breaching of the walls of Jerusalem by the Babylonian and the Roman armies, and the fast of *Tevet* on which the start of the Babylonian siege is remembered. In Israel this is also observed as a day of remembrance for the six million Jews who died in the Nazi Holocaust. Elements of fasting include abstention from food and drink, from bathing, from making love, and from wearing leather. In general Judaism is not a particularly ascetic religion, but through this annual pattern of fasts, the pious Jew can discipline his physical nature and vicariously share in the disasters which have befallen the Jewish people throughout the ages.

From Birth to Death

From ancient times all Jewish boys have been circumcised. According to the tradition, the practice (known as the *Brith Milah*) goes back to the Patriarch Abraham. Today the operation is still performed eight days after the birth. The child is held firmly and the actual surgery is performed by a **Mohel**, a

professional circumciser. This is a job which requires considerable training. Just before it, the father makes a blessing:
"Blessed art Thou, O Lord our God, King of the Universe, who
hast sanctified us through Thy commandments and hast commanded us to make our sons enter the covenant of Abraham."[18]
To this, the assembled company respond, "Even as this child has
entered into the covenant, so may he enter into the *Torah*, the
marriage canopy and into good deeds." The child is given his
Hebrew name and the ceremony is generally followed by a party.
The practice of circumcision is deeply rooted in the community.
Secular Jews, too, will often circumcise their sons—though perhaps by a surgeon rather than at a religious ceremony.

The birth of a daughter is recorded by a short baby blessing
in the normal synagogue service. Compared with the celebration accompanying a circumcision, it is a small affair. In recent
years, largely as a result of the feminist movement, there have
been attempts to introduce a special service for baby girls to
celebrate their entry into the covenant. Although several alternatives have been proposed, few have as yet succeeded in cap-
turing the potent mixture of pain, blood, insecurity, joy, and
ancient symbolism of masculine circumcision.

If the baby boy is the firstborn of his mother, a further ceremony (*Pidyan Ha-Ben*) takes place a month later. According to
the tradition, the firstborn son belongs to God and must be
redeemed by his parents. This involves the symbolic payment of
a sum of money or a small article of silver to a priest. Priests
(kohens) have few functions in Judaism, but some members of
the community, including Jews with the surname Cohen, trace
their ancestry to the priestly families that served in ancient
Israel. At the ceremony, the father hands over the money and
the priest (kohen) holds it over the baby and says, "This instead
of that, this in commutation for that and this in remission for
that."[19] He then prays for the child and gives the traditional
priestly benediction. This ceremony is not practiced by Reform
Jews—partly because the Reform Jews are not convinced by
claims of priestly ancestry and secondly because it is seen as dis-
criminatory to little girls.

At the age of 13, a boy is obliged to fulfill all the commandments, and in the synagogue he is called up to read from the Torah *at the* Bar Mitzvah *ceremony.*

According to Jewish law, parents have an obligation to educate their children and boys, in particular, are expected to be learned in Orthodox circles. At the age of 13, the boy attains Jewish adulthood. From then on he is expected to keep the commandments and his presence in the synagogue counts towards the necessary quorum for worship. When he reaches this status, he is known as *Bar Mitzvah* (son of the commandment). Traditionally it simply involves the boy being called up in the synagogue to read from the *Torah* scroll. For an Orthodox child who is experiencing an intensive Jewish education, this is not difficult. Boys raised in Orthodox households tend to find it easy to read the Hebrew text, but special lessons help out those less familiar with the language, so that they can sing their "portions" with as much proficiency as their more observant fellows. Often the ceremony is accompanied by a lavish party. In general the religious establishment is embarrassed about this, but feels powerless to stop it. Disappointingly too, once the event is over, many boys feel no incentive to continue with their Jewish education.

Once the Reform movement preferred to keep both boys and girls in religious school until the age of 16, rather than hold *Bar Mitzvah* services. However, community pressure ensured that now both boys and girls have their own ceremony. Girls at the age of 12 become *Bat Mitzvah* (daughter of the commandment) and their event is identical in every respect to their brothers'. Among the Modern Orthodox, girls also have a ceremony, but they do not read from the *Torah* scrolls. The strictly Orthodox continue to do very little to mark a girl's coming of age. More than a mere concession, for Reform, Conservative, and Modern Orthodox alike, the *Bat Mitzvah* confirms contemporary views of Jewish women's roles in the community.

marriage

The next major life-cycle event is marriage. Jews have no tradition of celibacy and among the strictly Orthodox, young men and women tend to marry in their late teens or early twenties. It is quite usual for the parents to support the young couple until the husband has finished his Jewish education. Among the non-Orthodox things are not so straightforward. The young people go to secular universities and embark on lengthy professional training. Away from home and often detached from the community, they frequently choose non-Jewish marriage partners. Intermarriage is said to pose the greatest threat to the continuance of the Dispersion community in its present form today. In the United States in the late 1980s, more than half of marriages involving Jews were mixed marriages. Generally the children of such unions are not brought up as Jews and are lost to the community.

Some of the non-Jewish spouses do convert to Judaism. More often a Jewish boy falls in love with a non-Jewish girl. He wants to marry her, but he also wants to have Jewish children. The Orthodox accept converts, but insist that the conversion must be the result of a desire to be Jewish, not from a desire to be married. The Progressive movements, on the other hand, are more accommodating. Believing that if Judaism is to survive

then converts are to be welcomed, their synagogues and
Temples provide regular conversion courses. In consequence,
the vast majority of those converted to Judaism in this century
have come through the Progressive organizations. The problem
with this is that the Orthodox do not recognize these people as
Jews. As far as they are concerned, they are still Gentiles and, if
they are women, their children will also be Gentiles. Today there
are many members of Reform and Conservative synagogues who
perceive themselves as Jews, who bring up their children as
Jews, who are regarded as Jews in their own communities, but
who are seen as non-Jews by the Orthodox.

Nonetheless, provided the particular synagogue accepts
both partners as Jews, a Jewish wedding can be celebrated. This
takes place under a marriage canopy (*chupah*) with both sets of
parents supporting their children. A formal marriage contract
(*ketubah*) is drawn up and signed by witnesses. Often these con-
tracts are beautifully illustrated, and are treasured as a keep-
sake by the couple. These days increasing numbers of Jews enjoy
customizing their own *ketuboth*, by incorporating artwork which
reveals aspects of their two personalities. In this way they can
create a uniquely personal item which affirms their faith in each
other, and in Judaism. Then the bride and groom drink from a
glass of wine and the bridegroom puts the wedding ring on the
bride's finger, saying the words, "Behold thou art betrothed to
me with this ring in accordance with the Law of Moses and
Israel".[20] This is followed by seven benedictions in which blessings are asked for the young couple and the ceremony concludes
with the bridegroom stepping on a glass and breaking it. The
origin of this custom is obscure, but it is thought to be a
reminder that even during the joy of a wedding, the destruction
of Jerusalem must not be forgotten.

A Jewish wedding is the cause of tremendous rejoicing. To
quote one of the blessings, marriage is regarded as a state of
"Joy and gladness, laughter and exaltation, pleasure and
delight, love, peace and friendship." Judaism does recognize
divorce, but it is regarded as a tragedy and Jews are known for
their strong family life.

Finally life has to come to an end. The tradition emphasizes that the utmost regard and consideration should be shown to the dying. They should be urged to make their final confession to God and ideally their last words will be those of the *Shema* ("Hear O Israel, the Lord our God, the Lord is One").[21] According to Jewish law, the body must be buried as soon as possible after death and the general principle is that the dead must be honored. The body must never be left alone. Among the Orthodox, it is ritually washed and buried in a simple linen or cotton shroud and the coffin contains no metal. The rabbi leads the funeral procession to the cemetery and prayers are said while the coffin is lowered into the ground and the grave filled. Generally a eulogy is made extolling the virtues of the deceased and finally the *Kaddish*, a prayer of praise of God and for peace, is recited.

Once the funeral is over, the family returns home to begin a seven day period of mourning. This is known as sitting *Shiva*. During this week, visitors from the community come to express their condolences and the family does not leave the house except perhaps to go to synagogue. During this time the mourners should recite the *Kaddish* three times each day to coincide with the daily services. Then, for the next 30 days, there is a time of lesser mourning when the *Kaddish* continues to be said, but the mourners gradually resume their regular routines. In the case of parents, *Kaddish* is said for a full year. Since it can only be said in a quorum of ten men, attendance at synagogue is mandatory during this period. Subsequently, every year, the dead person is remembered on the Hebrew date of his or her death. This death anniversary is known as the **Yahrzeit** and the practice is to light a candle which burns for the full day. Thus, in the Jewish tradition, the memory of those who have died is kept alive in the minds and hearts of those who loved them by a regular annual ritual.

By contrast with the Orthodox, Reform Jews occasionally choose to be cremated. Nonetheless the practices of saying *Kaddish* occasionally and lighting a *Yahrzeit* candle are widely observed even among the most secular.

The Future Hope

The strictly Orthodox continue to perceive the future in religious terms. Through the long centuries of exile from the Promised Land, the Jewish people hoped and prayed for signs that God would intervene in world history. Central to these beliefs was the coming of God's anointed King, the Messiah. According to the Psalmist in the Bible, God promised that King David and his descendants would rule over Israel for all time.[1] The last Davidic King was removed from the throne by the Babylonians in 586 B.C.E. Increasingly God's pledge was seen as a prediction of the future. God Himself would establish His sovereignty over the world; truth and justice would reign and this rule would last forever. Belief in the future Messiah was the twelfth of Maimonides' principles of the faith and the philosopher insisted that anyone who had doubts about him contradicts the *Torah*.

In the long course of Jewish history, there have been many messianic claimants. The best known are Jesus of Nazareth (first century C.E.), the founder of Christianity, Simeon bar Kokhba (second century C.E.), who led a rebellion against the Romans in 132 C.E., David Alroy (twelfth century), who led the Jews of Baghdad to believe that they would all fly to Jerusalem on the wings of angels, and Shabbetai Zevi (1626–76), whose career has already been discussed in Chapter 4. An important messianic candidate has also appeared in recent years. Menahem Mendel Schneersohn (1902–94), the leader of the *Lubavitcher Hasidim*, was perceived by many of his followers to fulfill the messianic prophecies. However, the vast majority of Jews, Orthodox, Reform, and secular alike, reject this claim. Even after his death, many of his devoted disciples were convinced that he would return again.

Over the centuries there has been much discussion as to what will happen when the Messiah does arrive. The rabbis of the *Talmud* believed that he would usher in a golden age, a time of total happiness. As God's chosen agent, he would restore justice, teach the *Torah*, and right all wrongs. The Twelve Tribes of the Israelite people would miraculously be gathered together again in the Land of Israel and all nations would look to Jerusalem for spiritual enlightenment. Thus the Zionist movement was a serious problem for the strictly Orthodox. According to the traditional scheme of things, the Jews were not meant to return to the land before the coming of the Messiah. In effect the Zionists despiritualized the promise of the return and saw the establishment of the Jewish State as a political rather than a religious goal. Today, there are still a few, very Orthodox, groups who do not accept the legitimacy of the State of Israel. Some may even live in the land, but they take no part in the political process and they continue to wait for divine deliverance. The majority of the Orthodox community, however, perceive the new State as the start, but not the fulfillment, of the messianic age. In view of the current state of affairs in the Middle East, this position becomes increasingly difficult to sustain since a major characteristic of the days of the Messiah is that there will be universal peace.

At the other end of the religious spectrum, the leaders of the Reform movement in the nineteenth century also rejected the messianic hope but for different reasons. They insisted that the Jews were not a nation but a religious community, and they considered the idea of the Messiah as too particularist and nationalistic. Instead, they understood the messianic age as a time of truth, justice, and peace which would be achieved by education, economic reform, and scientific discovery. The Holocaust finally convinced the Reform establishment of the Zionist cause. While supporting Israel, in general Reform congregations remain committed to social action as the divinely ordained means of transforming the world. In this century, Reform lawyers have been in the forefront of the Civil Rights cause; they have thrown their weight behind the liberation of women and they have been closely involved in the various peace movements. Thus the old expectation of God establishing His kingdom has been transformed into a secular commitment to social, political, and educational reform.

Traditionally the Jewish hope for the future was centered on this world—that the King-Messiah would establish God's Kingdom on earth. And, if it did not occur in one's own lifetime, then it would happen in the days of one's children or one's children's children. A doctrine of personal immortality only began to develop in the fourth or third century B.C.E., possibly as a result of Babylonian influence. It was not accepted by everyone. Even in the first century C.E., while the Pharisees insisted that the doctrine of life after death was implicit in the Scriptural texts, the Sadducees continued to reject it. By the twelfth century, however, a belief in the final resurrection of the dead was so established that it is listed as one of Maimonides' principles of the Jewish faith. The idea, as taught by the rabbis of the *Talmud*, was that in the Messianic Age, the dead would rise from their sleep and would be judged before God. Maimonides himself thought that after the resurrection, those who had been judged would die again and it was only the souls of human beings that were immortal.

Today most religious Orthodox Jews would agree with him. The modern understanding of scientific matter makes a physical resurrection difficult to accept. Nonetheless, belief in a final reward and punishment is an integral part of the tradition. In the past, it was generally agreed that the righteous would enter Heaven. This is described in the literature as being a place of beauty and delight. Meanwhile, those who have been rejected by God will be subjected to a series of appalling tortures. The notion of divine judgment is an essential component of the liturgy for the New Year and the Day of Atonement. However, modern Jews have, in general, rejected the idea of divine punishment. In his commentary on the traditional Prayer Book, the late chief rabbi of the British Commonwealth, J.H. Hertz, unequivocally asserted that "Judaism rejects the doctrine of eternal punishment" and that "Many and various are the folk beliefs and poetical fancies... but our most authoritative religious guides however proclaim that no eye has seen, nor can mortal fathom, what awaiteth us in the Hereafter; but that even the tarnished soul will not forever be denied spiritual bliss."[2] This seems to be a serious omission. If the wicked are not to be punished and all, in the end, are to be rewarded, it is hard to recognize the ultimate justice of God.

Thus the Jewish belief in the future is obscure. The strictly Orthodox continue to pray that God will send His Messiah to bring in the final golden age, to gather in the remnants of the Jewish people, to resurrect the dead and to exercise final judgment. The vast majority no longer expect this. The Reform and the Conservative believe that the soul is immortal, but they are not precise in their teaching. In particular, they have rejected the idea of eternal torment and many go still further. Many do not expect God ever to make His presence manifest in the world and they have lost all belief in personal immortality. The focus of their Jewishness lies either in their loyalty to the political State of Israel or in an abstract commitment to the survival of the Jewish people. These have become the twin pillars of modern Judaism—Israel and Jewish continuity. Many commentators do not believe that they will be enough to sustain Jewish identity through the next millennium.

The Survival of the Jewish State

Modern Israel, the Jewish State, was not created by the Messiah. It was the result of massive Jewish immigration, sympathetic world opinion, and a resolution of the United Nations. From its earliest days it has been in peril. When the United Nations recommended in 1947 that there should be a Jewish State, the surrounding Arab nations were determined that it should not be in their territory in the Middle East. In the War of Independence, the Jewish settlers were fighting against a vastly larger force, and even when the Arabs were defeated, they refused to recognize the new State's existence. In effect, Israel was under siege. Between the end of the War of Independence in 1948 and 1993, more than 18,000 Israelis had been killed in battle or been the victim of terrorist attack. In addition, world opinion turned against Israel during that period. In 1975 the United Nations condemned Zionism as a form of racism and increasingly the Israeli army was seen as an oppressive, imperialistic force.

The Palestinian problem has not gone away. After the Six Day War of 1967, the Israelis occupied the West Bank of the Jordan river and Gaza. These were the homes of millions of hostile Arabs—refugees from the Israeli War of Independence—most of whom lived in poor housing and had few educational opportunities. New Jewish immigrants were encouraged to settle in these territories. In 1982, the army tried to root out the Palestinian terrorists once and for all by attacking their bases in Lebanon. This campaign did nothing to restore Israel's image in the eyes of the world, particularly after the inhabitants of a Muslim refugee camp were massacred by Lebanese Christian soldiers, who were in alliance with Israel. Meanwhile the Arabs living in the occupied territories became more and more militant. The *Intifada* (popular insurrection) which began in 1987 was difficult to control. Even the most Israel loving Dispersion Jew was disturbed by pictures of Israeli soldiers firing at children throwing stones.

This is the background of the current peace initiative. In 1993, the then Israeli Prime Minister, Yitzhak Rabin (1922–96), himself a military hero, symbolically shook hands with Yassir Arafat (b.1929), the leader of the Palestinian Liberation Organization (P.L.O.). Both sides committed themselves to the Oslo Accords, which included the idea of Palestinian autonomy over Gaza and areas of the West Bank. The P.L.O. recognized Israel and Israel recognized the right of the P.L.O. to represent the Palestinians. Israel needed economic stability. For too long the country had been dependent on American support. In the early 1990s, 10 percent of the population was unemployed. With the advent of democracy in Russia, thousands of Russian Jews were exerting their right under the Israeli Law of Return to emigrate to Israel. Many of these people were highly educated. It was becoming increasingly necessary to develop an economy which could make use of their technological expertise. If Israel was to establish its own identity as an independent, economically stable country, peace was a necessity.

Even the assassination of Rabin by an extremist student, and the election of a rightwing government, has not killed the peace process. The Israeli right are supported by the ultra-Orthodox who are determined to establish a "Greater Israel" based on the boundaries promised by God in the Bible. Among the rest of the population, it is accepted that this is not realistic. The hordes of new Russian immigrants have all suffered from anti-semitism, but few have any knowledge of the Jewish religion, after 80 years of Soviet rule. A large proportion do not qualify as Jewish by the traditional Orthodox definition. What they want is to live decent lives and to enjoy economic and political stability. Even excluding the Russians, the majority of the Israeli population is not religious. Peace, not a "Greater Israel," is their priority.

Meanwhile people of Arab origin who have Israeli residence and Israeli citizenship comprise at least 20 percent of Israel's population. Their birthrate is also higher than the Jewish average. The majority are regarded as second class citizens by their Jewish neighbors and they are underrepresented in the universities and the professions. It is questionable how much longer they will tolerate this. Autonomous Palestinian regions have already been set up in the territories occupied by Israel since 1967 as a result of the peace process. It is likely that there will soon be an independent Palestinian State. It may be that the Israeli Arabs will be willing to move into the new country, but it is equally probable that they will prefer to disrupt the Jewish State with their own nationalistic aspirations. Recent events in the old Yugoslavia illustrate the possible dangers.

Many of the surrounding Arab countries see peace with Israel as the first step in creating a regional economic common market. On both sides there is an enormous incentive to establish a common trading alliance. For this to be successful, both Jewish and Muslim extremists will have to be sidelined. Once the Israelis are cooperating with the Jordanians, Syrians, and Lebanese on economic projects, many commentators believe that social interaction will follow. At present marriage is a problem in the Jewish State for anyone who cannot demonstrate an Orthodox Jewish maternal line. Very many of the Russian, Ethiopian, and American Reform immigrants have difficulties in this regard. Marriage continues to be controlled by the Orthodox establishment who will only authorize marriages of one Jew (by their definition) to another. Already this is the cause of much discontent. It will get worse once there are Israeli/Arab economic ventures since Jewish/Muslim marriages are likely to follow. In the same way as young Jews in the Dispersion are increasingly choosing their spouses from among the Gentiles with whom they have grown up and been educated, the same trend may well occur in Israel in the future.

Thus many observers believe that Israel will become just one nation among many in the Middle East. No longer will it be a Western outpost largely supported by American money, with its own unique and exclusive religion and culture. It will become part of the greater fabric of Middle Eastern society. By the end of the twenty-first century, the probability is that there will be a cultural blending between Jew and Arab. Israel will be largely a secular State. The strictly Orthodox will continue to inhabit their own self-imposed ghetto, but, despite their prolific birthrate, they will be only a small minority in the population. The vast majority will be secular Middle Easterners, descendants of both Jews and Arabs, dedicated not to the *Torah* and *Talmud*, but to prosperity and technological progress. It may be that the Orthodox will turn out to have been right after all—perhaps it is impossible to establish a Jewish State without the advent of God's Messiah. At the same time there have, in recent years, been hopeful developments in the world of Christian/Jewish relations. In 1965 the Roman Catholic Church issued the decree *Nostra Aetate*. In its section on the Jewish religión, it recognizes the spiritual bonds which link Jews and Christians and affirms God's continuing covenant with the Jews. Crucially, it absolves the Jews from the charge of having been God's killers: "True the Jewish authorities and those who followed their lead, pressed for the death of Christ; still what happened in his passion [his suffering and death]cannot be charged against all Jews without exception, then alive, nor against the Jews of today."[3]

Similarly the World Council of Churches, perhaps the most important of the Christian ecumenical bodies, in 1948, formally declared its abhorrence of the extermination of the Jews in the Holocaust. In 1948 motions were passed emphasizing the Jewishness of Jesus and God's concern for the Jews. In 1967 a statement was issued affirming that although God's revelation in the Hebrew Scriptures was fulfilled in Jesus, God did not abandon the Jewish nation. Today many countries support active Councils of Christians and Jews, which encourage encounter and dialogue between the two faiths. Although anti-semitism has been a constant feature in the history of Christendom, there are now signs that people of good will are trying to put aside this fearful tradition. There is evidence at last that Christians and Jews are beginning to appreciate the promise in the Psalmist's words: "Behold how good and pleasant it is for brethren to dwell together in unity ..."[4]

Judaism and Feminism

A large proportion of world Jewry no longer expects the Messiah to come and has little confidence in God's ultimate justice. It is likely that Israel itself will change from a Jewish State to a secular, Middle Eastern power. Many Jews are choosing to marry non-Jews and better relations are being forged between the Jewish and Christian religious establishment. There is another, even more serious challenge, to the traditional Jewish faith; it comes from the changing role of women in the world today.

Strict Orthodox Judaism is essentially a patriarchal religion in which men and women have clearly defined roles. Admittedly Jewishness itself is passed down from mother to child, but the child itself is always described as son or daughter of the father (as in Isaac *Ben* Abraham and Michael *Bat* Sha'ul). As we have seen, the birth of a son is traditionally a matter of great celebration with the ritual circumcision and possibly a Redemption of the Firstborn ceremony. The birth of a daughter is marked only by a short blessing during the course of a normal synagogue service. Thus it is made quite clear to everyone which gender is preferred by the Orthodox. This discrimination continues throughout childhood. The education of a boy is regarded as an important parental duty from which no effort must be spared. The child must grow up learned in *Torah* and *Talmud* to be a credit to his family. The education of a daughter is a different matter for the Orthodox. Certainly she must be wise in the ways of running a *kosher* home, but traditionally she is not encouraged to be an intellectual. In many circles women are not even permitted to study the *Talmud*. Although Orthodox communities in Israel and the United States do run religious schools for women, there are no women rabbis in the Orthodox community. When a boy reaches religious maturity at the age of 13, his *Bar Mitzvah* is a great event. Before his extended family, his parents' friends and the whole congregation, he is called up to read from the *Torah* scroll. There is no parallel service for girls in the tradition. It is recognized that girls mature earlier than boys, so a Jewish young woman becomes *Bat Mitzvah* at the age of 12, but probably the occasion is marked only by a little party at home.

Women are exempt from all the timebound positive commandments so they are not expected to take an active part in the liturgical life of the synagogue. Their presence does not even count towards the necessary quorum for worship. This means that if a woman's parents die and she has no brothers, she must either ask her husband or pay some other pious Jewish man to say *Kaddish* for the deceased. If she does attend synagogue herself, she has to sit in the women's area. This is either behind a heavy screen so she cannot see what is happening or way above the service in a separate gallery. Neither position encourages direct participation. In any event, her status is made clear during the course of the liturgy. Every day in the service the men pray, "Blessed art Thou, O Lord our God, King of the Universe, who hast not made me a woman."[5] The equivalent prayer for women is "Who hast made me according to Thy Will."[6]

Marriage and motherhood are the only acceptable destiny for a strict Orthodox girl. There is no parallel to the Christian monastic tradition where a particularly pious, talented, or intellectual young woman can develop her own interests and cultivate a personal relationship with the Almighty. In the 16 volumes of the *Encyclopaedia Judaica*[7] there are remarkably few entries for women. Only three books in the Hebrew Bible are named after women—Ruth, Esther, and Judith. In general, women are only remembered as the wives or mothers of male heroes or scholars. Since women are encouraged to marry young and birth control, at any rate in the early years, is strongly discouraged, they have little chance of completing a university education or embarking on serious professional training. According to the Book of Genesis, woman was created to be a "helpmeet" for man.[8] This has been understood to mean that the wife was to free her husband from all domestic cares so he was able to immerse himself in *Talmudic* scholarship. Over the centuries, female talent in the Orthodox world has been submerged in a welter of household cares.

Little has changed in today's strict Orthodox communities of Europe, the United States, and Israel. Boys are still educated separately from their sisters; early marriage for both sexes is very much encouraged and a large family is still regarded as a blessing. In general, the strictly Orthodox have dealt with the challenge from the feminist movement by ignoring it. In the

State of Israel, because the Orthodox have complete control in matters of personal status, women continue to find themselves with certain civil disabilities. Most acute is the matter of divorce. There is no civil divorce and, according to Jewish law, divorce can only be given by a man to a woman, not the other way round. If a man refuses to divorce his wife, she has no legal redress. She may find herself tied to a wife beater, a child molester, or a mass murderer, but if he will not give her the necessary document, she cannot be legally free of him. However, in other respects, women are not bound by Orthodox law. The constitution of Israel guarantees the complete equality of men and women. Among the vast majority of the Israeli population, daughters and sons receive the same education and enjoy the same professional opportunities.

Thus in the State of Israel, secular Jewish women find themselves in a strange position. On the one hand, they suffer a huge civil disadvantage in the matter of divorce, but in normal, everyday life, they can expect equality of treatment with their male colleagues. In the Dispersion, it is different. The vast majority of Jews are not affiliated with the strictly Orthodox. In Modern Orthodox synagogues women can and do assume positions of leadership. They are synagogue presidents and leading fundraisers. Nonetheless, it is impossible for them to be ordained as rabbis and they are not even counted among the necessary quorum for worship. This is because the Modern Orthodox believe that both the Written and Oral Law were directly given by God and therefore cannot be changed in any particular.

Things are very different in Conservative and Reform synagogues. There the women and men sit together and everyone takes a full part in the service. A Reform, Conservative, and Reconstructionist *Bat Mitzvah* is celebrated with the same excitement as a *Bar Mitzvah* and girls have exactly the same religious schooling as their brothers. Since the early 1970s, the Reform movement has ordained women as rabbis and, more recently, the Conservatives and Reconstructionists have followed suit. While the Conservative movement has accepted women's ordination and liturgical equality it is a hotly debated

Traditionally only men could serve as rabbis. However, in the last few decades women have been ordained as rabbis by the Reform, Conservative, and Reconstructionist movements.

issue in individual synagogues and the actual practice of synagogues with regard to egalitarianism varies a great deal. Today non-Orthodox rabbinical colleges have approximately equal numbers of men and women students and it is generally agreed that the caliber of the young women coming forward is often higher than that of the young men. It is likely, then, in the twenty-first century, that many of the leading pulpits will be occupied by female rabbis.

Modern Jewry has been strongly influenced by the feminist movement; indeed many of the best known feminist leaders are themselves of Jewish origin. Among the non-Orthodox and among secular Jews, the traditional passion for *Talmudic* study has been transformed into a desire that their children should enjoy the very best secular education that the Gentile world can offer. They want this for their daughters just as much as for their sons. Today there are large numbers of Jewish young women studying medicine or law, or who are attending business school. Their aspirations have been aided by positive discrimination in favor of women in the educational institutions themselves. Among this highly educated group, late marriage is the norm. In fact, many choose never to get married at all and there seems to be a serious shortage of young men of equal or superior accomplishment. Even if they do marry, they are most unlikely to have more than two children. The birthrate among non-Orthodox Jewish couples is low, way below the basic regenerating level.

Despite the efforts of the Modern Orthodox and the non-Orthodox synagogues, many of these clever, high-earning young women do not seem to be attracted to what is on offer. Even if they find a Jewish man to marry and they raise Jewish children, it is probable that their connection with the religious community will be tenuous at best. They will move easily in mainstream Gentile society and it is likely that many of their friends will be non-Jews. For young people brought up with and educated among the Gentile elite, intermarriage and complete assimilation is an ever present likelihood.

Assimilation and the Long-term Future

The American Jewish community remains the largest in the world and is richer and more powerful than ever before. The days of private clubs and certain housing areas being closed to Jews are over. From the early 1960s, Jewish young people have been moving in unprecedented numbers into the more prestigious universities and the professions. Their progress has been astonishing. By 1970, a quarter of the undergraduates at Harvard University were of Jewish origin as were 40 percent of those at Columbia. This generation of students grew up to have considerable influence in the legal and political circles of the 1990s. President Clinton (b.1946) appointed two Jews to the Supreme Court during his first administration, and in the Congress elected in 1992, Jews were represented in both houses in a proportion five times greater than their proportion in the population as a whole. It is the same story in medicine, in academia, in the entertainment industry, in journalism, in banking, and in business generally.

By 1994, American Jews formed less than 2 percent of the United States population, but they exerted influence in almost every public sphere. The community was overwhelmingly suburban, middle class, college educated and affluent. Significantly, from being traditionally liberal in politics, many became Republican in the Reagan/Bush era although the vast majority voted for the Democrat Bill Clinton. In the 1980s, however, economic self interest proved to be more powerful than the traditional Jewish emphasis on social justice and concern for the more disadvantaged members of society. In recent years, perhaps, things have been less rosy for the young. Programs of ethnic and sexual positive discrimination have been disadvantageous to Jewish male students (but not to their sisters). It may be that the generation growing up in the 1990s will have greater difficulty reaching the upper echelons of American society. Nonetheless, at present, the Jewish community appears to be doing very well.

This is not to say that anti-semitism no longer exists in the United States. But there is little evidence of it in polite society. The Holocaust illustrated all too clearly where Jew-hatred could lead. Through educational programs, Holocaust memorials and museums and in the artifacts of popular culture, the Nazi period is still successfully kept in the public eye. Films such as *Sophie's Choice* and *Schindler's List* ensure that the suffering of the Jews is not forgotten. The Anti-Defamation League, an organization founded to combat manifestations of anti-semitism, has been particularly effective in combating the expression of anti-Jewish prejudice. Even the recent outbreak of signs of anti-semitism in the African-American community has done little to harm the security of the community.

Inevitably, with the decline of overt Jew-hatred and with the entrance of Jews to all the institutions of American upper middle class life, Jews are regarded as desirable marriage partners. The figures speak for themselves. Between 1900 and 1940, less than 3 percent of married Jews were wedded to Gentile partners. The figure rose to 6.7 percent for those who married in the 1940s and 50s. By 1970, the figure had leapt to 31.7 percent and from the mid 1980s, it reached 52 percent.[9] In other words, for every Jewish couple getting married, there are two mixed couples. In the past Jewish men were far more likely to "marry out" than Jewish women. The pattern seems to have been that Jewish men who chose Gentile wives generally picked women whose fathers were of a lower socioeconomic standing than their own families. Many such women were willing to convert to Judaism. Today, at best only one in three spouses convert and less than one in three children of these mixed marriages are raised as Jews. The majority of these families are lost to Judaism. In addition, many Jews choose not to marry or prefer a homosexual partnership. In view of all this, many commentators believe that American Jews are, in the words of the historian Norman Cantor, "on a one-way ticket to disappearance as a distinctive ethnic group."[10]

The community is attempting to redress the situation. The figures indicate that it is Jews with little religious background who are more inclined to "marry out." There has been an explosion in the funding of Jewish day schools and synagogue programs to bring in the intermarried and unaffiliated. Meanwhile, the strictly Orthodox, who do seem largely immune to the effects of secularization, figuratively barricade themselves into their own observant ghetto. They are the only members of the community who are producing large numbers of children. The world of orthodox *Yeshivot* and girls' seminaries has never been so thriving. At the same time, the strictly Orthodox are cooperating less and less with the rest of the Jewish world, which they see as irredeemably assimilated. Yet even with this small, thriving enclave, the average number of children per Jewish family is way below the 2.3 needed to sustain the current population.

The situation is the same in the other countries of the Dispersion. The strictly Orthodox continue to maintain their particular way of life, but elsewhere in the community, the intermarriage rate grows and thousands of Jews are lost yearly. In Great Britain, for example, more than half of Jewish young people choose Gentile marriage partners and the rate of fertility of Jewish couples is at least 20 percent below that of the country as a whole. So great is the sense of urgency, that Jonathan Sacks (b. 1948), Chief Rabbi of the British Commonwealth, has written a book entitled *Will We Have Jewish Grandchildren?* [11] and has spearheaded a communitywide campaign for Jewish continuity.

Thus many observers believe that there are no grounds for optimism. The birthrate of Jews in the Dispersion is too low and the attractions of assimilation are too great. Admittedly, Israel will remain in the hands of people who are descended from Jews, but increasingly some commentators believe that in future decades they too will intermarry with the surrounding nations and will perceive themselves as Israelis rather than as Jews. The only survivors will be the strictly Orthodox, who will continue to worship the God of their ancestors as their parents did before them, but will be increasingly isolated from modern civilization.

Notes

Chapter 1

1   Adapted from Dan and
    Lavinia Cohn-Sherbok, *The
    American Jew* (London:
    HarperCollins, 1994. Grand
    Rapids: Eerdmans, 1995),
    pp.180–1.
2   Samson Raphael Hirsch, *The
    Nineteen Letters on Judaism*,
    as quoted in Lavinia and
    Dan Cohn-Sherbok, *A Short
    Reader of Judaism* (Oxford,
    One World, 1996), p.138.
3   G. W. Plaut, ed., *The Growth
    of Reform Judaism:
    American and European
    Sources*, as quoted in Cohn-
    Sherbok, *A Short Reader*,
    p.135.
4   The Passover ***Hagaddah***
    (many ed.).
5   *Kiddushin* III.
6   *Yebamot* XLVII.
7   Israeli Statutes: the Law of
    Return as quoted in Cohn-
    Sherbok, *A Short Reader*,
    p.170.
8   Statistics based on those cited
    in the *Encyclopaedia

Judaica as quoted in Cohn-
    Sherbok, *A Short Reader*,
    p.164.
9   Nicholas de Lange, *Atlas of
    the Jewish World* (Oxford,
    1984), p.174.

Chapter 2

1   Genesis 17:10–12.
2   Exodus 2:8.
3   Principles of the Jewish
    Faith as translated in the
    *Authorised Daily Prayer
    Book* (many ed.).
4   Psalm 89:4.
5   Ezekiel 34:12–13.
6   Exodus 29:9.
7   Exodus 20:8–10.
8   Romans 15:24.
9   Matthew 23:15.
10 Matthew 27:25.

Chapter 3

1   Sir Paul Ricaut as quoted in
    Cohn-Sherbok, *A Short
    Reader,* p.111.

2   Moses Mendelssohn,
    Jerusalem, as quoted in
    Cohn-Serbok, *A Short
    Reader*, p.130.
3   Theodor Herzl, *The Jewish
    State*, as quoted in Cohn-
    Sherbok, *A Short Reader*,
    p.141.
4   Adolf Hitler, *Mein Kampf*, as
    quoted in Cohn-Sherbok, *A
    Short Reader*, p.154.
5   Psalm 122:6.

Chapter 4

1   Deutreronomy 4:35.
2   Genesis 1:1.
3   Isaiah 55:8–9.
4   Psalm 145:9.
5   Job 38:4.
6   Exodus 19:5.
7   *Authorised Daily Prayer
    Book.*
8   *Ibid.*
9   *Ibid.*
10 Leviticus 19:27.
11 Numbers 15:37–8.
12 Genesis 6–9.
13 Exodus 23:19, 34:26;
    Deuteronomy 14:21.
14 Genesis 2:1–3.
15 Deuteronomy 16:16.

16 Passover *Hagaddah.*
17 Moses Maimonides, *Mishneh
    Torah* (many ed.).
18 *Authorised Daily Prayer
    Book.*
19 *Ibid.*
20 *Ibid.*
21 *Ibid.*

Chapter 5

1   Psalm 89:4. Also Samuel 2:7.
2   *Authorised Daily Prayer
    Book.*
3   The Vatican, *Nostra Aetate*
    (1965).
4   Psalm 133.
5   *Authorised Daily Prayer
    Book.*
6   *Ibid.*
7   (Jerusalem: Keter, 1971).
8   Genesis 2:18.
9   Figures taken from Jack
    Wertheimer, *A People
    Divided* (New York: Basic
    Books 1993), p. 59.
10 Norman Cantor, *The Sacred
    Chain* (New York, London:
    HarperCollins, 1994), p.
    426.
11 (Essex: Vallentine Mitchell,
    1994).

Glossary

Agudat Israel Orthodox organization set up to oppose Zionism.

Amidah Prayer consisting originally of 18 benedictions recited at the daily synagogue services.

Anti-semitism Hatred of the Jews.

Ark Original container for the tablets of the law; cupboard in synagogue in which the *Torah* scrolls are kept.

Ashkenazim Jews who settled in Northern France, Germany, and Eastern Europe, and their descendants in Israel and the USA.

Assimilation The loss of Jewish identity in mainstream Gentile culture.

Av 9 Fast commemorating the loss of the Jerusalem Temple.

Bar Mitzvah The coming-of-age ceremony for a boy at 13 years.

Bat Mitzvah The coming-of-age ceremony for a girl at 12 years.

Blood Libel Accusation that Jews murder Christian children and use their blood in the making of Passover unleavened bread.

Canon The established books of Scripture.

Chief Rabbi Established central religious authority of a particular community.

Chosen People Jews believe that they were chosen by God to keep His *Torah*.

Conservatives A modified reforming movement within American Judaism.

Covenant Special agreement between God and the Jewish people.

Crusade Medieval Christian movement to evict the Muslims from Palestine.

Day of Atonement Most holy day of the Jewish year which involves a daylong fast and prayers for forgiveness.

Dead Sea Scrolls	Collection of ancient scrolls probably produced by the Essenes.
Dispersion	The Jewish communities living outside the Land of Israel.
Enlightenment	The secular scientific and educational revolution of the late eighteenth, early nineteenth centuries.
Essenes	Monastic communities of Jews who flourished in the first century C.E.
Exegesis	Interpretation of sacred texts.
Exilarch	Head of Babylonian Jewish community from first to thirteenth centuries C.E.
Fast	Day of abstention from food.
Fringes (*tzitzit*)	Ritual tassels attached to the corners of garments.
Gaon	Title of the heads of the Babylonian *Talmudic* academies.
Gentile	Non-Jew.
Ghetto	Place set aside for Jewish residence.
Gospel	Christian story of the life and work of Jesus Christ.
Hagaddah	The order of service of the Passover meal.
Halakhah	Jewish law.
Hanukkah	Winter festival celebrating the victory of the Maccabees over the Hellenizers.
Hasidim	Adherents of an eighteenth-century Eastern European mystical movement.
Hellenizers	Those who tried to introduce Greek ideas in the fourth century B.C.E.
High Priest	The Israelite Chief Priest who served in the Temple in Jerusalem.
Holocaust	The destruction of European Jewry between 1933 and 1945.
Holy of Holies	The deepest sanctuary of the Jerusalem Temple.
Humanistic Judaism	A radical movement within modern American Jewry.
Intermarriage	Marriage between a Jew and a Gentile.
Israelites	The Jewish people particularly in Biblical times.

Kaddish	Prayer extolling God's greatness said by mourners.
Karaites	Adherents of an heretical sect founded in the eighth century C.E.
Kashrut	The laws governing food.
Kibbutz	An Israeli agricultural collective.
Kippah	Skull cap.
Knesset	The Israeli elected assembly.
Kosher	Fit to eat. Conforming to the laws of Kashrut.
Law of Return	The law which gives every Jew the right to settle in Israel.
Lulav	Bundle of myrtle, palm, and willow branches that are used during the services on *Sukkot*.
Matrilineal	Descended from the mother.
Messiah	God's chosen King, who will establish His Kingdom on earth.
Mezuzah	Parchment scroll attached to the doorposts of a Jewish house.
Midrash	Rabbinic commentary on the Bible.
Mikveh	Community ritual bath.
Mishnah	Oral Law. Also the title of Judah ha-Nasi's second-century compilation of the Oral Law.
Mitzvah	Commandment.
Mizrakhi	A party founded for Orthodox Zionists.
Modern Orthodox	Adherents of a modernist movement within Orthodoxy.
Mohel	Ritual circumciser.
Monotheists	Those who believe in One God.
Nasi	Title of the leader of the Palestinian Jewish community from second to fourth centuries C.E.
New Testament	The concluding part of Christian Scripture describing the life of Jesus Christ and early Church history.
New Year	1st day of the month of Tishri, the start of the Ten Days of Penitence.
Oral Law	The oral interpretation of the Written Law, recorded in the *Mishnah* and *Talmud*.
Orthodox	Those who believe the Written and Oral Law were given by God and must be obeyed in every particular.

Passover	Spring festival celebrating the liberation of the Jews from slavery in Egypt.
Patriarchs	The forefathers of the Jewish people, Abraham, Isaac, and Jacob (Israel).
Pentateuch	The first five books of the Hebrew Scriptures, Genesis, Exodus, Leviticus, Numbers, and Deuteronomy.
Pesah	Passover.
Pharisees	A religious sect of the Second Temple era who were scrupulous in obeying both Written and Oral Law.
Phylacteries **(tefilin)**	Boxes containing parchment scrolls which pious Jews bind each day on their arms and foreheads.
Pilgrim **Festivals**	Passover, *Shavuot*, and *Sukkot*, so called because they were traditionally celebrated in Jerusalem.
Piyyutim	Poems which are used as prayers.
Poale Zion	A socialist movement within Zionism.
Pogrom	An attack, often against the Jews, in nineteenth- and early twentieth-century Russia and Poland.
Progressive	Non-Orthodox.
Promised **Land**	Israel. The land promised by God to Abraham and his descendants in the Bible.
Prophet	One who speaks the word of God. The classical Prophets are those whose words are preserved in the Bible.
Proselyte	Convert.
Purim	Festival celebrating the deliverance of the Jews of Persia as recorded in the Book of Esther.
Rabbanite	One who, in contrast to the Karaites, accepted the validity of the Oral Law.
Rabbi	A recognized Jewish teacher and spiritual leader.
Rav	Title given to Jewish teachers in Babylonia.
Reconstruc- **tionists**	Adherents of a radical twentieth-century Jewish movement who regard Judaism as an evolving civilization.
Reform	A Progressive denomination which has attempted to make Judaism compatible with modern historical knowledge.
Resurrection	The belief that the dead will rise from their graves to be judged by God.

Rosh Hashanah	The Jewish New Year.
Sabbath	Saturday, the day of rest.
Sadducees	Aristocratic priestly sect in the days of the second Temple.
Samaritans	Descendants of the inhabitants of the Northern Kingdom who intermarried with the surrounding peoples.
Sanhedrin	Supreme religious assembly of the Jews at the time of the Second Temple and later.
Scroll	Rolled length of parchment on which the Holy Books are written.
Seder	Passover meal.
Selihot	Penitential prayers composed by the *Ashkenazim*.
Sephardim	Jews of Spanish or Oriental origin.
Septuagint	Third-century B.C.E. Greek translation of the Hebrew Scriptures.
Shabbat	Follower of the seventeenth-century false Messiah, Shabbetai Zevi.
Shabbos	The Sabbath.
Shavuot	Festival celebrating the giving of the *Torah*.
Shema	The primary declaration of the Jewish faith.
Shiva	Seven day period of mourning after the death of a close family member.
Shofar	Ram's horn trumpet blown on *Rosh Hashanah* and *Yom Kippur*.
Shtetl	Eastern European village inhabited mainly by Jews.
Sukkot	Festival commemorating the Jews' wanderings in the wilderness.
Synagogue	House of worship.
Tabernacles	*Sukkot*.
Talit	Undergarment with fringes (tzitzit) worn by Orthodox.
Talmud	Compendium of Oral Law compiled in Palestine in the late fifth and in Babylon in the late sixth century.
Temple	Central shrine of ancient times; modern Reform Synagogue.
Ten Commandments	Ten laws given to Moses as recorded in Exodus 20:2–14.

Ten Days of Penitence	Period from *Rosh Hashanah* to *Yom Kippur*.
Torah	God's revelation to the Jews; Jewish law; the Pentateuch.
Torah Scroll	Scroll on which the Pentateuch is written.
Tsaddik	Hereditary *Hasidic* leader.
Wall	Remaining part of the Jerusalem Temple.
Weeks	*Shavuot*.
World Zionist Organization	Central Zionist group.
Written Law	The laws of the Pentateuch.
Yahrzeit	Anniversary of the death of a close relation.
Yarmulke	Skull cap worn by Jewish men.
Yeshiva (pl. Yeshivot)	*Talmudic* academy.
Yiddish	Language of Eastern European Jewry.
Yom Kippur	Most important fast of the Jewish year.
Zealots	Jewish rebels against the Roman Empire.
Zionists	Those who are dedicated to restoring the Promised Land to the Jewish people.

This guide gives an accepted pronunciation as simply as possible. Syllables are separated by a space and those that are stressed are printed in italics. Letters are pronounced in the usual manner for English unless they are clarified in the following list.

a	fl*a*t	yoo	*you*
aa	f*a*ther	u	b*u*t
ai	th*e*re	ă	*a*bout (unaccented vowel)
ee	s*ee*	ch	*ch*urch
e	l*e*t	ġ	*g*ame
ī	h*i*gh	j	*j*et
i	p*i*ty	kh	guttural aspiration (ch sound in
ō	n*o*		Hebrew and German)
o	n*o*t	sh	*sh*ine
oo	f*oo*d	ts	car*ts*

Agudat Israel: ah ġoo *dat* iz
   raa ăl
Amidah: ah mee *dah*
Ashkenazim: ahsh ke *nah*
   zeem
Av: *ahv*
Bar Mitzvah: bahr mits *vah*
Bat Mitzvah: baht mits *vah*
Gaon: ġai ōn
Gentile: jen *tīl*
Hagaddah: hah ġah *dah*
Halakhah: hah lah *khah*
Hanukkah: *hah* nă kah

Hasidim: ha *sid* eem
Havdalah: hahv dah *lah*
Kaddish: kah *dish*
Kashrut: kahsh *root*
kibbutz: ki *boots*
Kippah: kip *ah*
Knesset: *kne* set
kosher: *kō* sher
Lulav: *loo* lahv
Maskilim: mah skee *leem*
mezuzah: me zoo *zah*
Midrash: mi *drahsh*
Mishnah: mish *nah*

mitzvah: mits *vah*
Mizrachi: miz rah *khee*
Mohel: mō *hel*
Nasi: *nah* see
Pentateuch: *pen* ta tyook
Pesah: *pe* sah
Pharisees: *far* i seez
phylacteries: fa *lak* tar eez
Piyyutim: pee yoo *teem*
Poale Zion: po *al* e tsī ōn
Purim: poo *reem*
rabbi: *ra* bī
Rav: *rahv*
Rosh Hashanah: *rōsh* hah
shah *nah*
Sadducees: *sad* yoo seez
Selihot: să *lee* hōt

Sephardim: se fahr *deem*
Shabbatean: shah *baht* ee an
Shabbos: *shaa* bos
Shavuot: shah voo *ot*
shema: shă *mah*
Shiva: *shee* vah
shofar: sho *fahr*
Shtetl: *shtet* ăl
synagogue: *sin* ah ġoġ
Talmud: tahl *mood*
Torah: tō *rah*
Yahrzeit: *yahr* tsīt
Yarmulke: *yahr* măl kă
Yeshiva: yă *shee* vah
Yom Kippur: *yōm* ki *poor*
Zealot: *zel* ăt

List of Festivals and Fasts

SEASON	DATE	FESTIVAL
Spring	*Nisan* 15–22	Passover—celebration of the liberation from slavery in Egypt.
	Iyyar 5	Israel Independence Day.
	Shivan 6–7	*Shavuot* commemoration of the giving of the Law to Moses on Mount Sinai.
Summer	*Tammuz* 17	Fast of *Tammuz*—remembering the breaching of the Jerusalem walls by Babylonians in 586 B.C.E. and Romans in 70 C.E.
	Av 9	*Tishah B'Av*—mourning the destruction of the Jerusalem Temple in 586 B.C.E. and 70 C.E.
Autumn	*Tishri* 1–2	*Rosh Hashanah*—the New Year in which Jews are called to repentance.
	Tishri 10	*Yom Kippur*—the Day of Atonement. The day is dedicated to prayer and fasting to atone for sin.
	Tishri 15–21	*Sukkot*—the feast of tabernacles in which Jews live in booths to remember their sojourn in the wilderness.
	Tishri 20–21	*Simhat Torah*—the Rejoicing in the Law. The annual cycle of *Torah* readings concludes and begins anew.
Winter	*Kislev* 25–*Tevet* 3	*Hanukkah*—Festival of Lights, celebrating the defeat of the Hellenizing king by Judas Maccabeus.
	Tevet 10	Fast of *Tevet*—remembering the start of the Babylonian siege and the victims of the Nazi Holocaust.
	Adar 14	*Purim*—commemorating the foiling of plans to destroy Persian Jewry as described in the Book of Esther.

These festivals and fasts are all described in Chapter 4.

Suggested Further Reading

General

Encyclopaedia Judaica. 16 Volumes (Jerusalem: Keter, 1971)
    Invaluable articles on every aspect of Judaism.
NICHOLAS DE LANGE, *Judaism* (Oxford: Oxford University Press, 1987)
    A popular, clear, and readable introduction to Judaism.
LOUIS JACOBS, *The Jewish Religion: a Companion* (Oxford: Oxford
    University Press, 1995)
    An excellent comprehensive introduction to the Jewish religion.
GEOFFREY WIGODER, *The New Standard Jewish Encyclopaedia* (rev. ed. New
    York, Oxford: Facts on File, 1992)
    A concise encyclopedia of Jewish religion and civilization.

Chapter 1

BARRY CHAMISH, *The Fall of Israel* (London: Canongate, 1992)
    An account of big business and Israeli corruption in the 1980s.
DAN AND LAVINIA COHN-SHERBOK, *The American Jew* (London:
    HarperCollins, 1994. Grand Rapids: Eerdmans, 1995)
    A snapshot of a modern American Jewish community.
YAEL DAYAN, *My Father, His Daughter* (New York: Farrar, Straus, 1985)
    A fascinating portrait of Israeli hero Moshe Dayan by his daughter.
DAVID ENGLANDER, ed., *The Jewish Enigma: an Enduring People* (London:
    Peter Halban, 1992)
    An overview of the community by a group of American and English
    scholars.
SANDER GILMAN, *The Jew's Body* (London: Routledge, 1992)
    A psychiatric interpretation of the role of anti-semitism in modern culture.

HYAM MACCOBY, *A Pariah People* (London: Constable, 1996)
An interesting anthropological explanation of anti-semitism.
AMOS OZ, *Israeli Literature. A Case of Reality Reflecting Fiction* (Colorado Springs: Colorado College, 1985)
Insights on Israeli culture by Israel's best known novelist.
NORMAN STILLMAN, *The Jews in Arab Lands in Modern Times* (Philadelphia: Jewish Publication Society, 1991)
A fascinating history of Jews in Islamic lands since 1800.

Chapter 2

RICHARD ELLIOTT FRIEDMAN, *Who Wrote the Bible?* (London: Cape, 1988)
A splendid summary of the findings of modern Biblical scholarship.
HANS KÜNG, *Judaism* (London: SCM Press, 1995)
An important book on early Jewish history written by the world's leading Roman Catholic liberal scholar.
JACOB NEUSNER, *The Bavli: An Introduction* (Atlanta: Scolars, 1992)
An indispensable guide to rabbinic Judaism written by a leading *Talmudic* scholar.
NORMAN STILLMAN, *The Jews of Arab Lands* (Philadelphia: Jewish Publication Society, 1979)
An excellent account of the history of *Sephardic* Jewry.
KENNETH STOW, *Alienated Minority: the Jews of Medieval Latin Europe* (Cambridge: Harvard University Press, 1992)
An interesting account of the medieval *Ashkenazic* community.

Chapter 3

MARTIN GILBERT, *The Holocaust: The Jewish Tragedy* (London: Fontana Press, 1987)
An overwhelming account of the twentieth-century Jewish tragedy. Gilbert is the official biographer of Winston Churchill.
BENJAMIN HARSHAV, *The Meaning of Yiddish* (Berkeley: University of California Press, 1992)
An important history of Yiddish culture and language.

IRVING HOWE, *The World of our Fathers: the Journey of Eastern European Jews to America* (New York: Schocken Books, 1990)
Bestselling account of the world of Eastern European Jewry.

MICHAEL MEYER, *Response to Modernity: History of the Reform Movement in Judaism* (New York: Oxford University Press, 1988)
A thorough history of the Reform movement.

ERNST PAWEL, *The Labyrinth of Exile: a Life of Theodor Herzl* (London: Collins Harvill, 1988)
An insightful biography of the founder of modern Zionism and his times.

Chapter 4

ISIDORE FISHMAN, *Introduction to Judaism* (London: Vallentine Mitchell, rev. ed. 1970)
A comprehensive introductory textbook of traditional Jewish belief and practice.

BLU GREENBERG, *How to Run a Traditional Jewish Household* (New York: Simon and Schuster, 1983)
A readable account of Modern Orthodox Jewish practice by a well-known Jewish feminist.

LOUIS JACOBS, *Principles of the Jewish Faith* (Northvale, New Jersey, London: Jason Aronson Inc. rev., ed. 1988)
An accessible exposition of Maimonides' Principles of the Jewish Faith by an eminent British scholar.

RICHARD SIEGEL, MICHAEL STRASSFELD, SHARON STRASSFELD, *The Jewish Catalog* (Philadelphia: Jewish Publication Society, 1973)
A bestselling do-it-yourself guide to Jewish practice.

LEO TREPP, *The Complete Book of Jewish Observance* (New York: Behrman House, 1980)
A useful, comprehensive guide to Jewish living.

Chapter 5

NORMAN CANTOR, *The Sacred Chain* (London: HarperCollins, 1994)
A splendidly iconoclastic view of Jewish history and the Jewish future.

JONATHAN SACKS, *Faith in the Future* (London: Darton, Longman and
Todd, 1995)
Reflections from the Chief Rabbi of the British Commonwealth on today's
moral issues in the light of Orthodox Judaism.

SUSAN WEIDMAN SCHNEIDER, *Jewish and Female* (New York: Simon and
Schuster, 1984)
A penetrating discussion of Judaism in the light of modern feminism.

STEPHEN SHAROT, *Messianism, Mysticism and Magic: A Sociological
Analysis of Jewish Religion* (Chapel Hill: University of North
Carolina Press, 1982)
A discussion of mystical and messianic beliefs by an Israeli sociologist.

BERNARD WASSERSTEIN, *Vanishing Diaspora* (London: Hamish Hamilton,
1996)
An examination of the recent history of the Jews of Europe focusing on
the possible extinction of a Jewish presence by the mid twenty-first
century.

Index